Excel

ADVANCED SKILLS

ENGLISH

YEAR 3

AGES 8–9

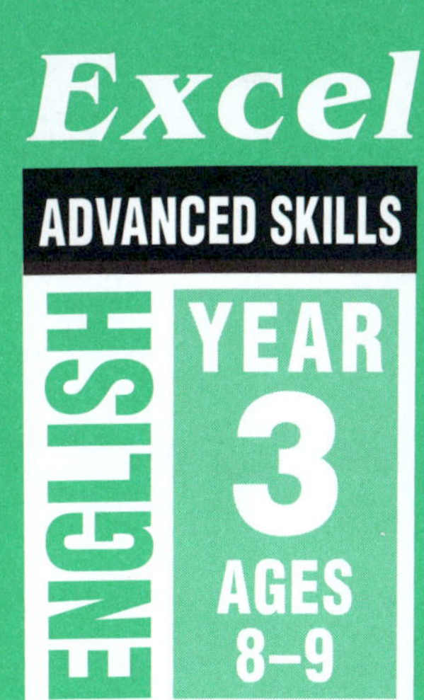

READING AND COMPREHENSION WORKBOOK

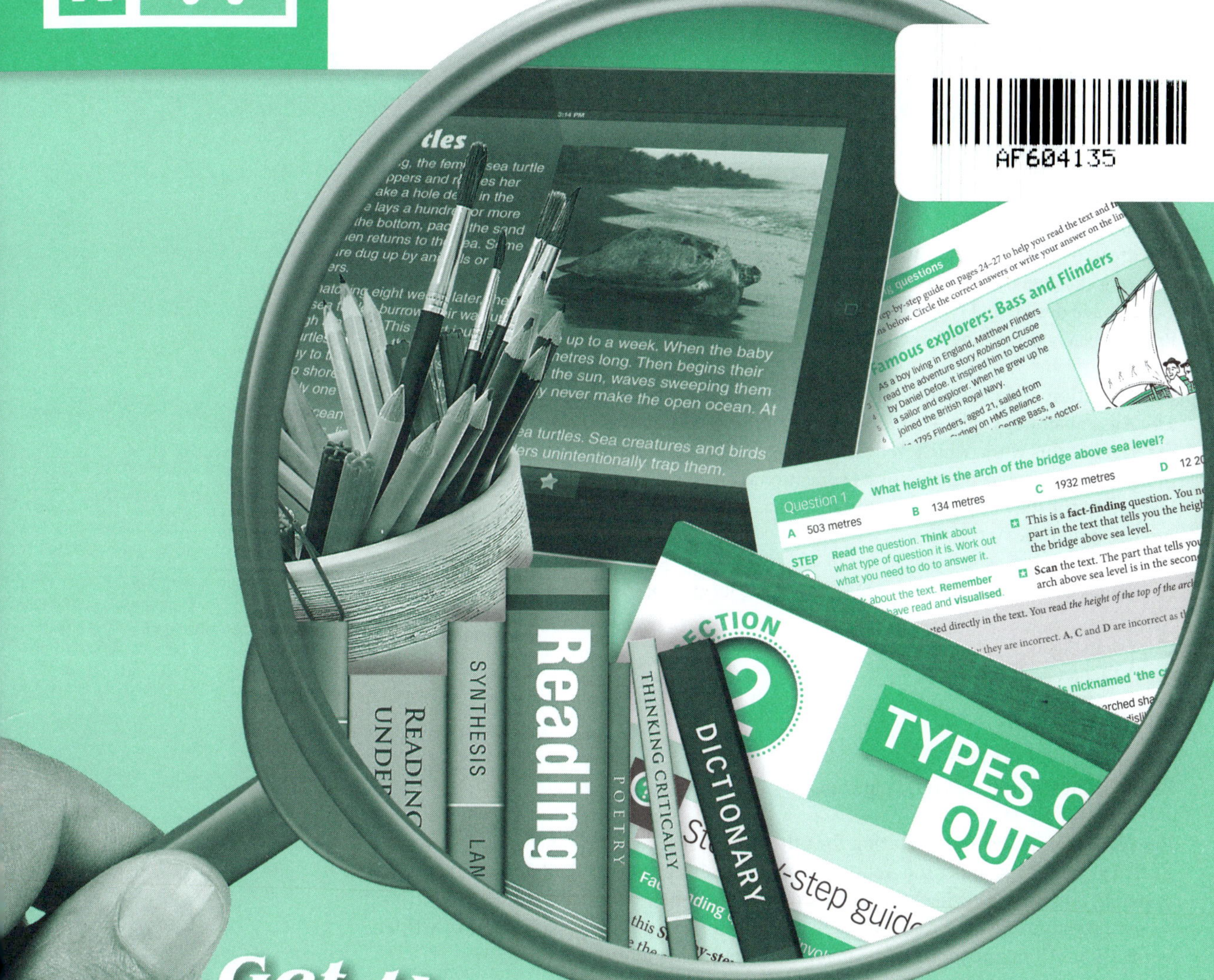

Get the Results You Want!

PASCAL PRESS

Donna Gibbs

Reprinted 2015, 2016, 2018, 2020, 2021

Updated in 2023 for the NSW Curriculum and Australian Curriculum Version 9.0 changes

Reprinted 2025

ISBN 978 1 74125 452 5

Pascal Press
PO Box 250
Glebe NSW 2037
www.pascalpress.com.au

Publisher: Vivienne Joannou
Project editor: Mark Dixon
Edited by Michael Wyatt
Proofread by Barbara Bessant and Mark Dixon
Answers checked by Glenda Walsh
Cover, page design and typesetting by DiZign Pty Ltd
Printed by Vivar Printing/Green Giant Press

CONTENTS

How to use this book

This book is designed to help students improve their reading comprehension skills and become more competent, reflective and critical readers.

It provides a step-by-step method of answering different types of comprehension questions, including those in standardised tests such as NAPLAN. Students are taught the strategies to read effectively.

The book is organised in four sections.

SECTION 1 Reading strategies

This section begins with a summary of the way the Step-by-step guide works for each type of comprehension question dealt with in this book. It defines the eight useful reading strategies frequently referred to. Once students have worked through Sections 1 and 2, they can use this guide to answer the mixed questions in Section 3.

Tips

- Make sure each student has ready access to the Step-by-step guide on page 4 as a useful reference when answering comprehension questions.
- Teach or revise the reading strategies of skimming and scanning, as well as ways to improve reading for understanding using the strategies of visualising, connecting, predicting, inferring, monitoring and judging (reading reflectively and critically).
- Have students complete the practice activities.

SECTION 2 Types of questions

This section deals with the five question types covered in the book. There is a chapter on each type: fact-finding, inferring, synthesis, language and judgement.

Each chapter begins with a sample reading text and step-by-step guide to reading that text and answering the particular comprehension questions.

There are five to six questions for each text. These are mostly multiple choice but at least one question per text requires a short written answer.

Tips

- Start with the chapter on fact-finding questions because these are usually the most straightforward questions to answer, depending on the complexity of the text. Judgement questions require higher-order thinking skills so they are dealt with last in the sequence here.
- Read and discuss the sample text at the beginning of the chapter. Point out the text's structure and language features. Discuss the content of the text and its purpose and audience.
- Talk to students about the type of question, how to identify it, what it's asking for and how to answer it. The Step-by-step guide makes clear to students the thought processes involved in reading with understanding.
- Discuss the strategies that competent readers use when reading a written text and answering comprehension questions.
- Discuss the answer explanations. These make it clear to students why their answers are correct or incorrect.

- Have students independently complete the comprehension tasks in each chapter.

Bringing it all together

Mixed questions

This section provides 18 reading texts with mixed question types for further practice.

Tips

- Have students complete the comprehension tasks independently in this section.
- Have students check their own answers and compare them with the answer explanations.

Answers

This section explains why answers are correct or incorrect. A suitable written answer is supplied for each short-answer question. The multiple-choice and short-answer questions enable the students to self-assess.

Tips

- Assess students' results. Analyse the patterns of correct and incorrect answers in students' results to identify areas of strength and weakness to assist with further development. Use this information to target and revise areas that need further attention.
- Identify the kinds of comprehension questions students are having difficulty with. Students for whom English is an additional language or dialect (EAL/D) often have most difficulty with inferring types of questions and questions which require background knowledge, or which use idioms that native speakers of English grow up using or knowing. English idioms can cause problems for many students, but especially students for whom English is a second language. Comprehension questions that depend on these concepts and ideas are specifically taught in the language questions section of this book.

Text overview grid

The Text overview grid on pages 122–125 provides a summary of the types of texts covered in the reading comprehension section of this book. It also offers additional teaching points and suggested ideas for student writing. Writing practice in different forms and genres will consolidate students' understanding of how texts are constructed and help them develop critical literacy.

Types of texts

The texts included in this book are defined according to their purposes: informative, imaginative and persuasive. Extracts from classic texts have been chosen to support the Australian Curriculum English Literature strand. Texts have also been chosen to support General Capabilities (Ethical Behaviour, Intercultural Understanding) and Cross-curricular Priorities (Aboriginal and Torres Strait Islander Histories and Cultures, Sustainability, Asia and Australia's engagement with Asia) of the Australian Curriculum.

READING STRATEGIES

Step-by-step guide

Reading the text

STEP		
STEP 1	**Skim** the text to see what it is about and how it is organised.	**Read** the title. Look at the illustrations and other visual elements. Make **predictions** about the subject and purpose of the text.
STEP 2	**Read** the text. **Monitor** your reading to make sure you understand it.	**Visualise** and **connect** with the ideas in the text**. Think** about what you already know about the subject and the type of text. Make **predictions.** Make **inferences**. Reflect on meanings and make **judgements**.

Answering specific types of comprehension questions

STEP 3 **Read** the question. **Think** about what type of question it is. Work out what you need to do to answer it.

- For a **fact-finding** question you need to find the part(s) of the text where the answer is stated directly. pp. 24–27
- For a **synthesis** question you need to think about how ideas and information relate to each other in a text. pp. 32–35
- For an **inferring** question you need to read between the lines to work out an answer that is not stated directly in the text. pp. 40–43
- For a **language** question you need to work out the meaning and effects of the language used in the text at the paragraph, sentence, clause and word level. pp. 52–55
- For a **judgement** question you need to make judgements about the information and ideas in the text, the writer's purpose and the values and attitudes embedded in the text. pp. 64–67

STEP 4 **Think** about the text. Remember what you have read and **visualised**. **Scan** the text to find the relevant parts. Look for key words or phrases. **Re-read** part or all of the text if necessary. Find answers stated directly in the text. **Infer** meanings or work out the answer using clues and evidence in the text and from your own knowledge. **Think** critically. Draw conclusions. Make **judgements**.

- For a **fact-finding** question scan the text to find the relevant parts. Look for words or phrases used in the question. Re-read parts of the text or the whole text if necessary, to find the answer.
- For a **synthesis** question scan the text to find the relevant parts. Look for words or phrases used in the question. Re-read parts of the text or the whole text if necessary. Draw together the threads of meaning and draw your own conclusions.
- For an **inferring** question scan the text for the relevant parts. Re-read parts of the text or the whole text if necessary. Use clues in the text to help you work out what is implied to answer the question.
- For a **language** question scan the text for the relevant parts. Re-read parts of the text or the whole text if necessary. Examine how language is used in context. Use your knowledge of language conventions, persuasive devices and figurative language to answer the question.
- For a **judgement** question scan the text for the relevant parts. Re-read parts of the text or the whole text if necessary. Think critically. Make judgements based on evidence in the text and your own knowledge and understanding to answer the question.

Terms used in the Step-by-step guide

Skimming

- Skimming over the text before you start reading tells you a lot about the text and how it is organised. Skim headings and subheadings. Look at visual elements. Predict the purpose and audience for the text.

  Good readers notice all of these things as they skim a text. pp. 6–7

Visualising

- Visualising (forming mental pictures) as you read helps you maintain focus during reading, connect to the meaning of the text and remember what you are reading about.

  Good readers visualise what they are reading about and store these images in their short-term memory. pp. 8–9

Connecting

- Connecting the text with your existing knowledge helps you make sense of the text. Think: How is this story like my life? What does this remind me of? What do I already know about this subject? Have I seen this kind of text before? Where? What do I recognise about the language of the text and its structures and features?

  Good readers connect to ideas in a text as they read. They relate new knowledge to existing knowledge and understanding about texts, themselves and the world. pp. 10–11

Predicting

- Making predictions about a text before you start reading as well as while you read helps you engage with the text. Predict what the text will be about. Predict the purpose and audience for the text. If you come across a word you are unfamiliar with, use the context to predict what the word could be and its likely meaning. Predict what will come next in the text.

  Good readers continually make predictions about a text and revise their predictions as they read. pp. 12–14

Inferring

- Making inferences as you read means working out what the writer is suggesting when it is not stated directly in the text. Writers often leave it up to the reader to read between the lines of a text. They give enough clues and contextual support for readers to be able to infer meanings. Sometimes writers leave meaning open to the reader's interpretation.

  Good readers make inferences as they read, reading between the lines to work out intended meanings in the text. pp. 14–16

Monitoring

- Monitoring your reading means thinking about the text as you read and making sure it makes sense. When you monitor your understanding of a text you realise very quickly when meaning breaks down. Re-read parts of the text to revise your understanding.

  Good readers monitor their reading to maintain meaning as they read. They read on, to confirm or refute predictions and inferences, then re-read and revise understanding when inferences don't make sense. They self correct. pp. 16–17

Judging

- Judging means thinking critically as you read. Judge the information and ideas in the text and the ways these are expressed or implied. Making judgements about a text is an important part of being critically literate.

  Good readers make judgements about a text, its context and its purpose as they read. Critically literate readers can judge whether a text is reliable, trustworthy, relevant, current, accurate, interesting, entertaining or useful based on their own purposes for reading. Critically literate readers can make judgements about the attitudes and values embedded in texts. pp. 18–20

Scanning

- Scanning means looking quickly through sections of a text for specific words, phrases or images.

  Good readers can quickly find what they need in a text without having to read whole texts or sections of text. pp. 21–23

Reading with understanding

This section provides practice activities for the eight strategies referred to in the **Step-by-step guide** on page 4. These strategies support reading with understanding and answering comprehension questions. They are:

1. Skimming
2. Visualising
3. Connecting
4. Predicting
5. Inferring
6. Monitoring
7. Judging (reading reflectively and critically)
8. Scanning.

Effective readers are able to use the strategies simultaneously without necessarily being aware that they are doing so. They make decisions about which strategies to use depending on the text and their purposes for reading.

① Skimming

What is it? **Skimming** is a useful quick 'first glance' strategy to get a general idea of what a text is about and how it is organised. Skimming a text's structure and features helps you to make predictions and judgements about the text before you read it.

When you skim a text you can often tell whether it is an informative, imaginative or persuasive text. You notice features such as lists, paragraphs, columns, photographs, art work, diagrams and maps. You can skim a text to judge whether you want to read it.

How do you do it? When you skim a text your eyes move quickly across and down, or zigzag over a text, stopping briefly at the parts that get your attention such as headings, words in bold or illustrations.

For example, you might:

- skim a notice attached to a bus shelter to see if it is a timetable or a notice for a garage sale
- pick up a book titled *The Sea*, thinking it is an information book, but a quick skim through it will show you it is a novel
- look for a report in the local newspaper about your school fete; you skim through the pages to find a relevant heading or a photo to locate the text you are searching for.

Have a go!

Skim the texts below. You don't need to read them. Just skim over each text's structures and features and identify what kind of text it is. Notice any visual elements. Work as quickly as you can. Choose a label from the box for each text.

poem   report   website   instructions

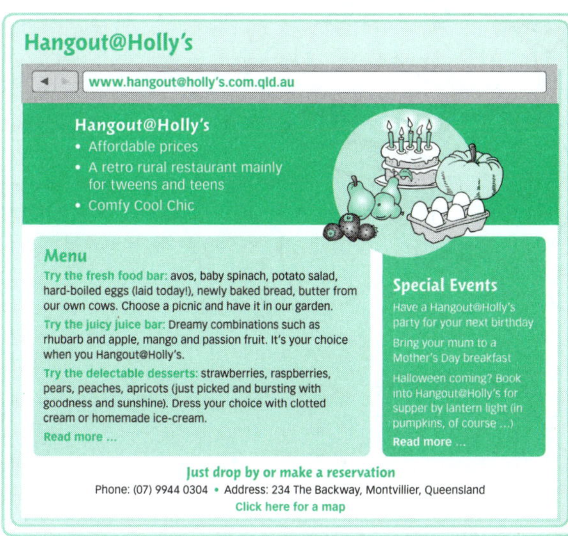

Hangout@Holly's

www.hangout@holly's.com.qld.au

Hangout@Holly's

- Affordable prices
- A retro rural restaurant mainly for tweens and teens
- Comfy Cool Chic

Menu

Try the fresh food bar: avos, baby spinach, potato salad, hard-boiled eggs (laid today!), newly baked bread, butter from our own cows. Choose a picnic and have it in our garden.

Try the juicy juice bar: Dreamy combinations such as rhubarb and apple, mango and passion fruit. It's your choice when you Hangout@Holly's.

Try the delectable desserts: strawberries, raspberries, pears, peaches, apricots (just picked and bursting with goodness and sunshine). Dress your choice with clotted cream or homemade ice-cream.

Read more ...

Special Events

Have a Hangout@Holly's party for your next birthday

Bring your mum to a Mother's Day breakfast

Halloween coming? Book into Hangout@Holly's for supper by lantern light (in pumpkins, of course ...)

Read more ...

Just drop by or make a reservation

Phone: (07) 9944 0304 • Address: 234 The Backway, Montvillier, Queensland

Click here for a map

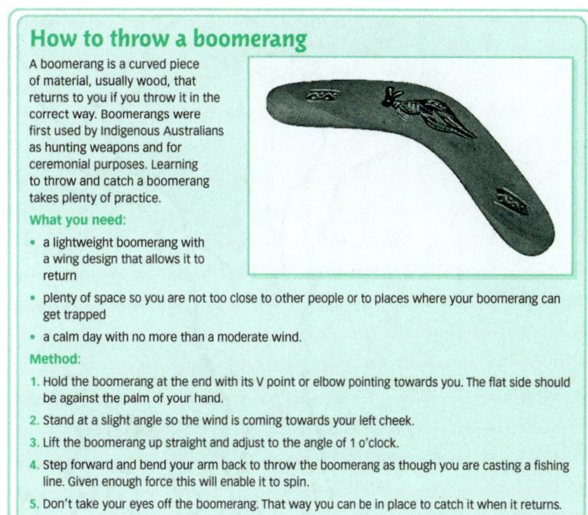

How to throw a boomerang

A boomerang is a curved piece of material, usually wood, that returns to you if you throw it in the correct way. Boomerangs were first used by Indigenous Australians as hunting weapons and for ceremonial purposes. Learning to throw and catch a boomerang takes plenty of practice.

What you need:

- a lightweight boomerang with a wing design that allows it to return
- plenty of space so you are not too close to other people or to places where your boomerang can get trapped
- a calm day with no more than a moderate wind.

Method:

1. Hold the boomerang at the end with its V point or elbow pointing towards you. The flat side should be against the palm of your hand.
2. Stand at a slight angle so the wind is coming towards your left cheek.
3. Lift the boomerang up straight and adjust to the angle of 1 o'clock.
4. Step forward and bend your arm back to throw the boomerang as though you are casting a fishing line. Given enough force this will enable it to spin.
5. Don't take your eyes off the boomerang. That way you can be in place to catch it when it returns.

A ....

B ....

Bees

Bees are flying insects. Like all insects, their bodies have three parts—a head, a thorax and an abdomen. They have five eyes, two sets of wings and three pairs of legs. The hair that covers a bee's body, including parts of its eyes, collects pollen. Bees scrape this pollen into pollen 'baskets' attached to the outsides of their back legs.

There are many different species of bees. Those that live in hives, such as the honey bee, make a honeycomb of cells inside the hive where they store nectar and the queen bee's eggs.

The queen bee is the 'head' of the society. She lays thousands of eggs. Drones, male bees, make up about five per cent of the bee community. Their main job is to mate with the queen bee. The workers, female bees, have different functions including making honeycomb cells for storage, feeding the queen bee and her larvae, keeping the hive clean and cool, and collecting nectar and pollen. They work hard and sometimes they literally die from exhaustion.

Scout bees search for the best places to find nectar. For bees to fill their stomachs with nectar, they have to visit about 2000 flowers. When they return to the hive they do a waggling dance that tells other bees where to go to find nectar.

When I grow up

When I grow up
I plan to be
someone who lives
by the sea.

I'll sail my boat
and surf and swim
eat fish and chips
to suit my whim.

Perhaps to keep me
out of debt
I'd learn to fly
an airline jet.

I could act in a film,
or drive racing cars
or turn astronaut and
zoom to the stars.

I could be a cop
or a very brave firey
Or live on the land
and own my own dairy.

I'd milk the cows,
have a tractor to drive.
Shear the sheep,
get honey from a hive.

Mum says, 'You're dreaming,'
and she's quite right.
Yet it's half the fun
on a cold winter's night.

It's far in the future
so I really don't know.
But I do like dreaming
about it so!

C ....

D ....

Answers

A You skim the layout and notice the visual elements and design. You notice the illustrations of fresh food. Hangout@Holly's is a website that advertises a restaurant.

B You skim the layout and notice the subheadings, the dot points and the numbered sentences. The text is a set of instructions for how to throw a boomerang.

C You skim the layout and note that it is in paragraphs. You notice there is a realistic photograph alongside the text. It is an informative report about bees.

D You skim the layout and notice that it is in verse. It is a poem about growing up.

② Visualising

What is it? **Visualising** means making mental pictures or picturing information in your mind as you read. Visualising helps you engage with a text so you understand it more readily and remember what you've read.

How do you do it? You picture in your mind what is described in the text.

For example, you could:

- read a factual description of an animal and visualise what it looks like
- visualise the setting described in a narrative
- read a recipe and visualise what the final product will look, smell and taste like when it is cooked.

Have a go!

Read the lines of text taken from *Just in Time* (Part 1) and then stop reading. Close your eyes and visualise what you have read.

A

> Every day, Tom crept through a hole in the fence to visit the kittens. Billy, an orange kitten, was the one he liked best. Billy liked to rub his nose against Tom's leg. He had a very loud purr!

What do you see? What's happening? Imagine it in motion like a film strip.

Now compare what you have visualised with the suggestion below.

Answer You see Tom creeping through a hole in the fence. When he reaches the kittens without being seen, he kneels down close beside them. His eyes look for Billy, his favourite. Billy rubs his nose against Tom's leg and starts to purr loudly. Tom looks contented and happy.

B

> One day, Tom hid Billy under his jumper and took him to school. He hid him in his desk. He took off his jumper and squeezed it into the desk as well. There was a round hole in the corner of Tom's desk where an inkwell used to sit. Billy could breathe through that. He was soon asleep.

What do you see? What's happening? Imagine it in motion like a film strip.

Now compare what you have visualised with the answer below.

Answer You see Tom walking to school trying to look as if everything is as usual. You notice there is a bulge in his jumper that is Billy. You watch Tom go into his classroom and secretly slide Billy from under his jumper into his desk. You notice that Tom's desk is the old-fashioned sort with an inkwell hole. You see Tom take off his jumper and push it into his desk for Billy to snuggle into. Billy goes to sleep and Tom relaxes because his kitten is safe and quiet.

C

> Mr Brown, Tom's teacher, was chalking some figures on the blackboard. The class was silent for once working at Maths. Mr Brown noticed a vibratory sound somewhere nearby and turned around.

What do you see? What's happening? Imagine it in motion like a film strip.

Now compare what you have visualised with the answer below.

Answer The scene moves from a close up of Tom at his desk to the whole classroom. Mr Brown, the teacher, is writing with chalk on an old-fashioned blackboard. The children are quietly doing Maths. There is hardly a sound to be heard. Then you hear a vibrating noise start up. You guess that Billy is purring loudly as you've learned he often does. You imagine Tom's heart sinking as he sees Mr Brown turn around. You see from the expression on Tom's face that he is hoping against hope Mr Brown does not try to find out where the vibrating sound is coming from.

③ Connecting

What is it? **Connecting** with a text means relating it to yourself, your life and the world in which you live. It means making connections between things you already know or know about and the new information in a text. Connecting helps you understand and remember what you read. Readers connect to texts in different ways based on their own life experiences.

How do you do it? As you read a text you make connections with your own knowledge and experiences. You connect with a text when you think things such as:

'This reminds me of ...'

'I saw something like that ...'

'I've read this kind of text before ...'

For example, you might:

- connect with characters in a story because you understand their feelings from experiencing something similar
- connect with outrage expressed about animal cruelty in a newspaper article because it engages your own strong feelings about animal welfare
- connect and pay close attention to information about a measles epidemic because you know that the girl next door has just caught the measles.

Have a go!

Read through the text. Make connections with the experiences that are described. Then answer the questions below.

'Sandy, hop up on the desk for me, please.'

They were having their Health lesson. It was part of Physical Education, which was Sandy's favourite subject.

'Now, put your feet together, Sandy. See there, girls and boys. See that space between Sandy's knees. That's the sign of having bowlegs. Bowlegs is a condition in which the knees stay wide apart when a person stands with their feet and ankles together.'

Sandy felt the blood rush to his cheeks and spread slowly over his whole body. This couldn't be happening. He didn't know where to look.

'You were all bow-legged until you began to walk,' Miss White added cheerfully. 'Once you are upright, your legs usually straighten up, but not always,' the teacher replied. 'Thanks, Sandy. You can get down. Now, what about tennis elbow. Who knows what that is?'

Sandy wished he could disappear. Simone guessed how he felt. She wanted to show him she understood but she didn't know how.

A Have you ever had any experiences or feelings similar to Sandy's or known someone who has? Explain.

....

....

....

B How do you feel about what Miss White did? Explain.

....

....

....

C Have you ever felt as Simone does? Did you find a way to express your feelings?

....

....

....

Compare your answers with these suggestions:

ANSWERS

A You might recall a time when you were unexpectedly embarrassed in front of other people. You may remember how you hoped no-one would notice your blushes or even the tears that sprang into your eyes. You may have watched someone else in this kind of situation and felt sorry for them.

B You are likely to disapprove of Miss White using Sandy to explain what *bow-legged* means. She may not have meant to be unkind because she goes on cheerfully without seeming to notice Sandy's embarrassment. However, you wish Miss White had understood that pointing out that Sandy was bow-legged in front of his classmates would be upsetting for him.

C Your own personality, background and experiences will shape your response to this question. You may recall wishing you could offer comfort to someone when you knew he or she was feeling upset, without further embarrassing them in front of others. You might have given them a friendly smile, asked them to join you and your friends in a game or found some other way to express your support.

④ Predicting

What is it? **Predicting** means thinking ahead as you read a text and guessing what might come next based on what you understand so far. Predicting makes you an active reader. It helps you connect to the text and remember what it is about.

How do you do it? As you read you use evidence in the text to make predictions. You can change your predictions as you read on and get new evidence.

For example you can predict:

- the contents of a book by skimming its cover
- what might happen next in a story
- the meaning of a word from its context or from reading on and finding out more
- the next word in a text using your knowledge of language patterns
- what an article in a newspaper is likely to be about from a photograph beside it.

Have a go!

1 Predict which words are missing from these sentences by using your knowledge of language patterns (grammar and vocabulary).

A The possum .... across the top of the fence towards the juicy passionfruit.

Answer Suitable verbs include 'ran', 'scampered' and 'tiptoes'. When you read the sentence you can predict that the missing word will be a verb and you can infer that the missing word's meaning is something to do with movement.

B The audience clapped .... when the concert ended.

Answer You can predict that the missing word is an adverb. The answer is 'loudly' or any adverb that tells you how they clapped at the end of the concert, such as 'enthusiastically', 'deafeningly' or 'half -heartedly'.

C He walked along the .... path towards the derelict house.

Answer Suitable words include 'winding', 'overgrown', 'uneven' or 'red'. When you read the sentence you can predict that the missing word will be an adjective and you can infer that the missing word's meaning will provide a description of the path such as its length, shape, quality or colour.

2 Read this story and make predictions to answer the questions below.

The train roared through the tunnel. Junior felt scared. He turned his head backwards and forwards trying to see where the sky had gone.

'Don't wriggle, Junior,' Mrs Pigeon said, nudging her young son with her rounded stomach. 'You'll draw attention to yourself.'

'Sorry, Mum,' Junior cooed. He'd never been on a train before. It was all very well for his parents. They often caught the train these days, saying it saved on energy now they were getting more elderly.

'Move closer, Junior. This is not our stop and others will be getting out.'

Junior watched hundreds of pairs of feet trudge carefully around his family and step down onto the platform.

'Next stop is ours. We'll be at the park all day but you can fly off with your friends' Mr Pigeon said, ruffling his son's feathers affectionately. 'Be back on the platform by 3 pm. We want to avoid the commuters on the way home.'

A When you read the first paragraph, what did you predict the story would be about?

....

....

Answer You are likely to have predicted the story is about a young boy who is afraid to be on his own in a dark tunnel.

B What did you read in the next paragraph that made you confirm or change your prediction?

....

....

Answer You realise Junior is with his mother so he is not alone. You read that she nudges him with her stomach. You wonder if she is a very large mother or there is some other reason for her nudging Junior like this.

C What do you read in the next paragraph that makes you confirm or change your prediction?

....

....

Answer The word cooed raises the possibility that Junior isn't a boy but a bird. It seems Junior might be having his first train ride with his parents and you predict they might be a family of pigeons rather than people.

D What do you read in the rest of the text that makes you confirm or change your predictions?

....

....

Answer You read that Mr and Mrs Pigeon often catch the train and they can read. This makes you doubt your prediction that they are really pigeons. Then you read that people step carefully around the trio as they step off the train, that Mr Pigeon ruffles his son's feathers, not his hair, and that Mr Pigeon tells his son he can fly off with his friends. Your earlier prediction is confirmed. You decide that the story is about a family of pigeons who regularly catch the train.

⑤ Inferring

What is it? You **infer** meaning when you work out what a writer is implying or suggesting without actually stating it directly in the text.

How do you do it? You think about meanings that are implied or hinted at. You read between the lines to work out what the author is implying or suggesting.

For example, you can

- infer from the order in which events happen how they relate to each other
- infer what characters think or feel from their interactions, from what they say to each other or what a narrator implies
- infer how writers feel about a subject from their choice of language.

Have a go!

Read each text and make inferences to answer the questions below.

1 Potatoes sometimes contain toxins produced in response to stresses to the plant. High levels of toxins are sometimes found in potato sprouts and potato peel that has a bitter taste. Cooking does not destroy the toxins and they can cause stomach ache and other problems.

What are toxins?

A vitamins **B** colours **C** healthy nutrients **D** poisons

Answer **D** is correct. You can infer that toxins are harmful so they are likely to be poisons. **A**, **B** and **C** are either not harmful to humans or are very unlikely to be of harm to them.

2 I remember my first tooth getting wobbly. Mum said she would tie one end of a cotton thread around it and tie the other end of the thread to the doorknob so she could pull it out for me. She went to get the cotton from her sewing kit. When she came back I was in my room under the bed.

'Tim,' she called. 'Where are you, dear?' I didn't answer. I didn't want to disappoint Mum but what else could I do?

Why doesn't Tim answer his mother?

....

....

Answer You infer that Tim doesn't like the idea of having his mum pull out his wobbly tooth so he hides under his bed, doesn't answer her and hopes she won't find him.

3 The second his mother parked in front of Grandpa's house, Harold jumped out of the back seat of the car. He walked around to the front and opened the car door for his grandfather and helped him out. Then he slid quickly into the front seat beside his mother.

Evan, Harold's twin brother, began his familiar complaint.

'It's not fair, Mum, Harold always …'

'Stop complaining, Evan,' his mother interrupted. 'Your turn next time.'

When would her boys ever grow up?

Why does Harold get out of his seat the second his mother stopped the car?

....

Answer You read Harold's mother ask when would her boys ever grow up? You can infer that Harold and his brother have competed over sitting in the front seat of the car in the past. You work out that Harold wanted to get out before his brother so he could be the one to open the door for his grandfather and then, more importantly in his mind, grab the front seat before his twin brother.

4 Tigers are the largest of the animals in the cat family. They are part of myth and folklore and often have an important role in stories and films. The tiger is a national symbol of several Asian countries including India, Vietnam and Malaysia. The image of the tiger appears on flags and coats of arms and it is a favourite symbol of sporting teams. And yet, over the last century tigers have suffered the loss of around 90 per cent of their habitats in the wild. This has led to their becoming an endangered species.

Question: What does the author imply has caused the loss of tiger habitats?

....

Answer You can infer that the author thinks humans are responsible for the loss of tiger habitats. The words *And yet* alert the reader to the idea that humans honour tigers yet, at the same time, they are the ones who allow them to become an endangered species.

⑥ Monitoring

What is it? **Monitoring** means noticing as you read when a text doesn't make sense. It means thinking about the meaning of what you are reading so you immediately notice when meaning breaks down or you lose the thread of a text.

Maintaining the thread and connecting meanings across a text is part of remembering and understanding what you have read.

How do you do it? As you read you ask yourself if what you are reading makes sense. You self-correct when meaning breaks down by re-reading previous sentences, sections of the text, or the whole text. You clarify things you might have misunderstood, misinterpreted or forgotten. As you read, if you need to, you adjust your predictions and rethink your inferences.

Have a go!

When you are reading for meaning you do not always need to read or decode every word. You can usually work out meanings when you read on and consider word use in the context of the sentence, the paragraph or the text as a whole.

Try this.

People often think that ostriches bury their heads in the sand. In fact, they don't. What deceives people is they use their beaks to turn over their eggs while they are acrobating.

You read: *to turn over their eggs while they are acrobating.*

If you are monitoring meaning as you read, you think about what *acrobating* means and whether this is something eggs would be likely to do. You decide that it doesn't make sense. You question the text. Why would ostriches' eggs perform acrobatics in their nest? You try to visualise eggs acrobating. That's not very likely. So you re-read the text.

This time you read *to turn over their eggs while they are incubating.*

You understand that you have misread 'acrobating' for *incubating*. You are not sure what *incubating* means so you read on.

Once the eggs have been sat on and kept warm in the nest for about six weeks, the baby ostriches hatch.

You work out that the meaning of incubating is being kept warm in the nest until the eggs hatch. This is quite different in meaning from 'acrobating'!

If you hadn't monitored the meaning of what you were reading, you would have held a very confused idea about the behaviour of ostrich eggs!

⑦ Judging

What is it? **Judging** a text means reading critically and reflecting on what you read. As you read, you make judgements about how information and ideas in a text are presented.

How do you do it? As you read, you evaluate whether the ideas and information are trustworthy, credible, biased, influenced by values and attitudes at the time something was written and so on.

For example, you can make judgements about:

- an informative text's trustworthiness for particular purposes
- a website's usefulness for particular purposes
- a character's behaviour in a story
- the time and place in which a text is set
- the bias of information in a persuasive text
- an author's attitude to such matters as gender, race and culture
- how effectively language is used in a text.

Have a go!

1 Read the text below and make judgements about its usefulness for the purposes listed.

> When nesting, the female sea turtle uses her flippers and rotates her body to make a hole deep in the sand. She lays a hundred or more eggs at the bottom, packs the sand back, then returns to the sea. Some nests are dug up by animals or poachers.
>
> After hatching eight weeks later, the baby sea turtles burrow their way up through the sand. This short journey can take up to a week. When the baby sea turtles emerge, they are about 4.5 cm long. Then begins their journey to the sea. Predators, dehydration in the sun, waves sweeping them back to shore and other dangers mean many baby sea turtles never make the open ocean. At best, only one in a thousand will survive.

Circle the correct answer. Is the text relevant to your needs if your purpose is:

A to find out about the migratory habits of sea turtles? Yes No Maybe

Answer No. The text does not have any information about the migratory habits of sea turtles.

B to collect information about sea turtles for a project? Yes No Maybe

Answer Yes. The text provides information that could be included in a project on sea turtles providing you can judge that the source is reliable.

C to find out if sea turtles are an endangered species? Yes No Maybe

Answer Maybe. The text includes some information about dangers to sea turtles' survival. This could be useful in understanding their endangered status. On the other hand, the text doesn't say anything directly about whether sea turtles' numbers have decreased and whether anything is being done about improving their chances of survival.

2 Make a judgement about the usefulness and trustworthiness of these websites for research into the topic of Australian symbols and emblems.

Which website(s) would you consider looking at?

A http://en.wikipedia.org/wiki/List_of_symbols_of_states_and_territories_of_Australia

B http://australia.gov.au/topics/australian-facts-and-figures/national-symbols

C www:kim'sozzieemblemblog.com

D http://www.dpc.wa.gov.au/GuidelinesAndPolicies/SymbolsOfWA/

....

Answer The most trustworthy of these websites for research into Australian symbols and emblems is likely to be the government website (**B**). You would judge it to have more accurate and unbiased information than a personal blog such as in website **C**. You would judge website **A**, the Wikipedia site about symbols of the states and territories, might be worth looking at but as Wikipedia articles can be written anonymously and by anyone, the information is not usually as trustworthy as that of more official sites. Website **D** is a government site but it relates to Western Australia only so will be less useful than a site which deals with Australian emblems and symbols more generally.

3 Read the extract from *The Railway Children* by Edith Nesbitt, written in 1905.

'I think we'd better keep it for a rainy day. In other words, I'll give up Saturday afternoon to it, and you shall all help me.'

'CAN girls help to mend engines?' Peter asked doubtfully.

'Of course they can. Girls are just as clever as boys, and don't you forget it! How would you like to be an engine-driver, Phil?'

'My face would be always dirty, wouldn't it?' said Phyllis, in unenthusiastic tones, 'and I expect I should break something.'

'I should just love it,' said Roberta—'do you think I could when I'm grown up, Daddy? Or even a stoker?'

'You mean a fireman,' said Daddy, pulling and twisting at the engine. 'Well, if you still wish it, when you're grown up, we'll see about making you a fire-woman. I remember when I was a boy—'

Just then there was a knock at the front door.

Use evidence from the text to judge what is unusual, in a story written more than a century ago, about the father's attitudes to bringing up children.

....

....

Answer Over a century ago people usually thought of male and female roles in a stereotyped way. For example, a woman's place was in the home. It was unusual for women to think about careers. Men had the breadwinner role. And if there was an engine to fix, it was a job for a male, and so on.

The father's attitude in this story is not like this. He teaches his children not to take any notice of stereotyped ideas about boys and girls. He treats his son and daughters as equals. He wants them to be whatever they want to be when they grow up. His ideas about gender are not at all stereotyped.

4 Read the text and make judgements to answer the questions below.

To the Editor

Recently I watched a video of a whale that couldn't swim properly, or raise itself from the water, because it was so entangled in metres of cast off fishing net. The whale was close to death. Luckily, a small group of people on a boat saw the distressed whale and after several hours of difficult, dangerous work managed to free it.

If you could have seen the whale's joy at being free you would have wept. It flung itself out of the water in sheer joy, again and again. I counted about forty breaches before it headed off into the deep. It left me feeling helpless and sad about the damage we do to marine animals through our careless behaviour.

Yours sincerely

Ben Stratter

Is Ben's letter likely to help the cause of whale conservation? Circle your choice of answer and explain the reasons for your judgement.

A definitely **B** possibly **C** probably not **D** definitely not

....

....

Answer You are likely to choose either **B** or **C**. You judge that the way Ben describes the plight of the trapped whale is very moving and possibly could inspire people to look into how they can help change human behaviour that threatens the lives of whales and other marine animals.

On the other hand, Ben says he feels helpless and doesn't make any suggestions about what could be done. This leaves people without ideas about what to do to help the whales. In this case you would judge his letter would probably not help the cause in any practical way.

Both **A** and **D** are unlikely answers because they express more certainty than is justified by the text.

8 Scanning

What is it? **Scanning** is a strategy that helps you find specific information in a text. When you scan a text you look quickly through it to find the particular things you want to locate.

When answering reading comprehension questions it is important to read the whole text first before attempting to answer any questions. Once you have read a text, scanning can be a useful strategy for locating the information you need to answer a question. If you scan the text for answers without reading the text you might overlook important information needed to answer a question accurately.

How do you do it? Look quickly through the text to find the part you need, then examine that area more closely.

For example, you can scan:

- a text you have already read for information you need
- an alphabetical index to find your name
- a list of ingredients in a recipe to see if a particular ingredient is included
- an invitation to a party to find its date and time
- a group photo for your image
- a graph for a particular item
- a map for a place name.

Have a go!

1 Read the extract from *Little Women* by Louisa May Alcott, written in 1868. Then scan the text to locate and re-read the part you need to answer the questions.

> Meg wanted a few curls about her face, and Jo undertook to pinch the papered locks with a pair of hot tongs.
>
> 'Ought they to smoke like that?' asked Beth, from her perch on the bed.
>
> 'It's the dampness drying,' replied Jo.
>
> 'What a queer smell! It's like burnt feathers,' observed Amy, smoothing her own pretty curls with a superior air.
>
> 'There, now I'll take off the papers and you'll see a cloud of little ringlets,' said Jo, putting down the tongs.
>
> She did take off the papers, but no cloud of ringlets appeared, for the hair came with the papers, and the horrified hair-dresser laid a row of little scorched bundles on the bureau before her victim.

A Who wanted to have her hair curled?

....

B What did the burnt hair smell like to Amy?

....

C What did Jo hope to see when she put down the tongs?

....

D What did she see instead?

....

Answers **A** Meg **B** burnt feathers **C** a cloud of little ringlets **D** a row of little scorched bundles

2 Read the texts through first. Then scan the text to locate and re-read the part you need to answer the question.

Hi Mum

This sounds like a great sale.

Can you meet me there next Thursday evening after work?

Love Sally

Save lots of $$$$$$

Mid-year sale at DYERMONES for our VIP customers.

Sale opens on 25th June and runs until June 30th.

Women's, men's and children's clothes reduced by up to 70%.

Homewares reduced by up to 50%.

Buy one pair of shoes and get one pair FREE.

Doors open at 9 am and close at 6 pm.

Late night shopping until 9 pm on Wednesday.

For more information email dyermones@oz.com.au

A Which store is advertising?

....

B Who is the sale for?

....

C What date does the sale begin?

....

D What date does it end?

....

E How can you contact the store?

....

F What is wrong with Sally's plan to meet her mum?

....

Answers **A** Dyermones **B** VIP customers **C** June 25th **D** June 30th **E** By email **F** Late night shopping for the sale is on Wednesday, not Thursday.

TYPES OF QUESTIONS

Step-by-step guide to **fact-finding** questions

Fact-finding questions involve finding information that is stated directly in the text.

Use this **Step-by-step guide** to help you read the text and **find facts** to answer the questions below. Circle the correct answers or write your answer on the lines.

STEP 1	**Skim** the text to see what it is about and how it is organised.	**Read** the title, *The Sydney Harbour Bridge*. Look at the illustrations and other visual elements. Notice what the illustration tells you about the kind of bridge it is. Notice that the text is written in paragraphs. Make **predictions** about the subject and purpose of the text.
STEP 2	**Read** the text. **Monitor** your reading to make sure you understand it.	**Visualise** and **connect** with the ideas in the text. **Think** about what you already know about the subject and the type of text, a report. Make **predictions.** Make **inferences**. Reflect on meanings and make **judgements**.

The Sydney Harbour Bridge

The Sydney Harbour Bridge is the tallest steel-arched suspension bridge in the world. The arch spans 503 metres, and the height of the top of the arch is 134 metres above sea level. The bridge is much admired by tourists and has been painted and photographed many times. People nickname it 'the coathanger' because of its shape.

Until 1932, when the Sydney Harbour Bridge was opened, getting from the city to the northern suburbs of Sydney was not easy. It meant catching a ferry or travelling by road for 20 kilometres and crossing five separate bridges.

Building the bridge took 1400 men eight years. Some 122 000 cubic metres of rock had to be excavated for the foundations. Its construction took 53 000 tonnes of steel and 6 000 000 hand-driven rivets. Painting the bridge took 272 000 litres of paint.

After the bridge opened, to cross it cost threepence for a horse and rider, and sixpence for a car. Two tracks were used for trams until the 1950s when Sydney closed down its tram service. Now trains, buses, cars, trucks, bikes and pedestrians use it daily. People used to pay the bridge toll to staff stationed in booths, but since 2009 tolls have been paid using an electronic computer system.

(Source of figures: Mackaness, C (ed.), *Bridging Sydney*, Historic Houses Trust of New South Wales, Sydney, 2006)

Question 1 What height is the arch of the bridge above sea level?

A 503 metres **B** 134 metres **C** 1932 metres **D** 12 200 metres

STEP 3 **Read** the question. **Think** about what type of question it is. Work out what you need to do to answer it.

This is a **fact-finding** question. You need to find the part in the text that tells you the height of the arch of the bridge above sea level.

STEP 4 **Think** about the text. **Remember** what you have read and **visualised**.

Scan the text. The part that tells you the height of the arch above sea level is in the second sentence.

B is correct. The answer is stated directly in the text. You read *the height of the top of the arch is 134 metres above sea level (see lines 4–5)*.

Check the other options to confirm why they are incorrect. **A**, **C** and **D** are incorrect as they name the wrong number of metres.

Question 2 The Sydney Harbour Bridge is nicknamed 'the coathanger' because

A it is made of steel coathangers.

B its arched shape is like a coathanger's shape.

C people like to hook firework displays onto it.

D people dislike the bridge and use this name to insult it.

STEP 3 **Read** the question. **Think** about what type of question it is. Work out what you need to do to answer it.

This is a **fact-finding** question. You need to look at the illustration of the bridge and find the part of the text that tells you why the Sydney Harbour Bridge is nicknamed 'the coathanger'.

STEP 4 **Think** about the text. Remember what you have read and **visualised**.

Scan the text. The part that tells you why people nicknamed the bridge 'the coathanger' is at the end of paragraph one. Compare this information with what the illustration tells you about the bridge.

B is correct. The answer is stated directly in the text. You read that it is a steel-arched bridge with a similar shape to a coathanger. You can confirm this by looking at the illustration. This is why people have given it this nickname.

Check the other options to confirm why they are incorrect. **A** is incorrect as coathangers were not used in the construction of the bridge. **C** is incorrect because, although the bridge is used for firework displays, its nickname of 'coathanger' has nothing to do with this. **D** is incorrect as you read the bridge is much admired.

Question 3 Before 1932, to get from the city to the northern suburbs by road meant people had to

A cross the Sydney Harbour Bridge.

B catch the tram over the harbour.

C drive 20 kilometres.

D drive through the Sydney Harbour Tunnel.

STEP 3 **Read** the question. **Think** about what type of question it is. Work out what you need to do to answer it.

This is a **fact-finding** question. You need to find the part of the text that tells you how people got from the city to the northern suburbs by road before 1932.

STEP 4 STRATEGY **Think** about the text. Remember what you have read and **visualised**.

Scan the text. The part that tells you how people got from the city to the northern suburbs by road before 1932 is at the end of paragraph two.

C is correct. The answer is stated directly in the text. You read *getting from the city to the northern suburbs … meant … travelling by road for 20 kilometres (see lines 10–12)*. Travelling by road involved this long drive as the Harbour Bridge was not opened until 1932.

Check the other options to confirm why they are incorrect. **A** is incorrect because the Sydney Harbour Bridge was not opened until 1932. **B** is incorrect as the tram tracks on the bridge were not available to use until after the bridge was opened in 1932. **D** is incorrect because the Sydney Harbour Tunnel is not mentioned.

Fact-finding questions involve finding information that is stated directly in the text.

The Sydney Harbour Bridge

The Sydney Harbour Bridge is the tallest steel-arched suspension bridge in the world. The arch spans 503 metres, and the height of the top of the arch is 134 metres above sea level. The bridge is much admired by tourists and has been painted and photographed many times. People nickname it 'the coathanger' because of its shape.

Until 1932, when the Sydney Harbour Bridge was opened, getting from the city to the northern suburbs of Sydney was not easy. It meant catching a ferry or travelling by road for 20 kilometres and crossing five separate bridges.

Building the bridge took 1400 men eight years. Some 122 000 cubic metres of rock had to be excavated for the foundations. Its construction took 53 000 tonnes of steel and 6 000 000 hand-driven rivets. Painting the bridge took 272 000 litres of paint.

After the bridge opened, to cross it cost threepence for a horse and rider, and sixpence for a car. Two tracks were used for trams until the 1950s when Sydney closed down its tram service. Now trains, buses, cars, trucks, bikes and pedestrians use it daily. People used to pay the bridge toll to staff stationed in booths, but since 2009 tolls have been paid using an electronic computer system.

(Source of figures: Mackaness, C (ed.), *Bridging Sydney*, Historic Houses Trust of New South Wales, Sydney, 2006)

Question 4 How many tonnes of steel did the construction of the Sydney Harbour Bridge take?

A 122 000 tonnes   B 53 000 tonnes   C 6 000 000 tonnes   D 272 000 tonnes

STEP 3 **Read** the question. **Think** about what type of question it is. Work out what you need to do to answer it.

This is a **fact-finding** question. You need to find the part of the text that tells you how many tonnes of steel the construction of the bridge took.

STEP 4 **Think** about the text, Remember what you have read and **visualised**.

Scan the text. The part that tells you how many tonnes of steel the construction of the bridge took is in paragraph three.

B is correct. The answer is stated directly in the text. You read *Its construction took 53 000 tonnes of steel* *(see line 15)*.

Check the other options to confirm why they are incorrect. **A**, **C** and **D** are incorrect because they give the wrong number of tonnes of steel used to construct the bridge.

Question 5 You could catch a tram across the Sydney Harbour Bridge

A between 1932 and the 1950s.
B only before 1932.
C after 1960.
D only in the 1930s.

STEP 3 **Read** the question. **Think** about what type of question it is. Work out what you need to do to answer it.

This is a **fact-finding** question. You need to find the part that tells you when you could catch a tram across the bridge.

STEP 4 **Think** about the text. **Remember** what you have read and **visualised**.

This is a **fact-finding** question. **Scan** the text. The part that tells you when you could catch a tram across the bridge is in paragraph four.

A is correct. The answer is stated directly in the text. You read *After the bridge opened … Two tracks were used for trams until the 1950s when Sydney closed down its tram service* (see lines 17–18). The bridge was opened in 1932 (paragraph two) and it had tram tracks. The tram service was closed down in the 1950s. This means you could get a tram across the bridge between these dates.

Check the other options to confirm why they are incorrect. **B** is incorrect as the bridge was not built at that time. **C** is incorrect because there have not been tram tracks on the bridge since before 1960. **D** is incorrect because you could also catch a tram across the bridge in the 1940s and part of the 1950s.

Question 6 How has the way people pay the toll to cross the Sydney Harbour Bridge changed?

Explain your answer on the lines below.

....

....

....

STEP 3 **Read** the question. **Think** about what type of question it is. Work out what you need to do to answer it.

This is a **fact-finding** question. You need to find the part of the text that gives information about changes to the way people pay the toll on the bridge.

STEP 4 **Think** about the text. Remember what you have read and **visualised**.

Scan the text. The part that tells you about changes to the way people pay the toll on the bridge is in the last sentence of the text.

The answer is stated directly in the text. You read that people used to pay staff stationed in booths but since 2009 tolls have been paid using an electronic computer system. This means that the change in how the toll is paid has been from paying a person—a toll collector—to payment being collected electronically by use of a computer system.

Fact-finding questions

Use the **Step-by-step guide** on pages 24–27 to help you read the text and **find facts** to answer the questions below. Circle the correct answers or write your answer on the lines.

Counting

When I was one
I had lots of fun.
When I turned two
I found plenty to do.
I liked being three
but four I liked more.
Being five was ok
and six not too bad.
Seven was great
but not better than eight.
Eight. Have you guessed?
I like it the best.
I like playing soccer,
I'm in the school team,
I have a new bike,
and it rides like a dream.
I do have some doubts
about turning nine.
Will the big kids be mean?
No ... It's sure to be fine.
I think you could say
I'm easy to please.
Or maybe it's simply
that life's the bees knees*!

by Tilly

**The bee's knees* means something that's really good.

1. At what age was Tilly when she had lots of fun?
   - **A** 1
   - **B** 2
   - **C** 3
   - **D** 4

2. Which is Tilly's favourite age?
   - **A** 5
   - **B** 6
   - **C** 7
   - **D** 8

3. How old is Tilly?
   - **A** 9
   - **B** 8
   - **C** 7
   - **D** 6

4. Tilly has some doubts about turning nine because
   - **A** she worries about everything.
   - **B** she wonders if the older children might be mean to her.
   - **C** she is afraid to grow up.
   - **D** she has never wanted to be nine.

5. What reasons does Tilly give to explain how she feels about her life?

....

....

....

....

Answers and explanations on p. 94

Fact-finding questions

Use the **Step-by-step guide** on pages 24–27 to help you read the text and **find facts** to answer the questions below. Circle the correct answers or write your answer on the lines.

Where to get your new pet

Dear Editor

I think people should get their pets from animal shelters or pet rescue groups. The big advantage is you save the life of a homeless animal that might otherwise die. You are able to offer the animal the chance of a good new life. The money used to pay to adopt your pet helps fund these organisations. This means more animals can be saved and cared for.

Animal shelters are often run by volunteers, which means they really care about the animals. Some shelters even have programs to match the personality of a pet with that of its new owner. 'Meet Your Match' is a program I tried and that's how I found Ruffie. Ruffie was rescued from a bushfire. We get along really well together.

Other advantages are:

- shelters get new animals every day so there's always plenty of choice
- you can be sure the animal's health has been checked and that they are vaccinated against diseases
- shelter animals cost less than animals from breeders or pet shops.

At least you should try a shelter before going elsewhere when looking for a pet. I don't think you'll be disappointed.

Yours sincerely

Ari Bejang

1. Where does Ari think people should get their pets? Choose all that apply.
   - **A** from pet stores
   - **B** from animal shelters
   - **C** from animal breeders
   - **D** from pet rescue groups
2. The money you pay to a shelter to buy your pet is used to
   - **A** only pay for pet vaccinations.
   - **B** help fund the animal shelter.
   - **C** pay the volunteers.
   - **D** pay to buy new animals.
3. 'Meet Your Match' is a program about
   - **A** matching a pet's personality with that of its new owner's.
   - **B** finding a pet that is healthy.
   - **C** matching people with work that suits them.
   - **D** matching pets with each other.
4. Shelter animals cost
   - **A** more than animals bought from pet shops.
   - **B** the same as animals bought from breeders.
   - **C** less than animals bought from pet shops.
   - **D** twice the price of animals bought from other places.
5. What does Ari recommend someone wanting a pet should do?

   Explain your answer.

   ....

   ....

   ....

   ....

   ....

Answers and explanations on pp. 94–95

Fact-finding questions

Use the **Step-by-step guide** on pages 24–27 to help you read the text and **find facts** to answer the questions below. Circle the correct answers or write your answer on the lines.

Famous explorers: Bass and Flinders

As a boy living in England, Matthew Flinders read the adventure story *Robinson Crusoe* by Daniel Defoe. It inspired him to become a sailor and explorer. When he grew up he joined the British Royal Navy.

In 1795 Flinders, aged 21, sailed from England to Sydney on HMS *Reliance*. On board, he met with George Bass, a childhood friend, and now the ship's doctor. They were both keen to explore new lands.

In 1796 they attached a mast to the *Tom Thumb*, a 2.5 metre rowing boat Bass had brought with him on the *Reliance*. On this tiny boat they explored and charted areas of the coastline in Botany Bay and the George's River.

In 1798, they circumnavigated* Van Diemen's Land (now called Tasmania) on the *Norfolk*, a ship built by convicts on Norfolk Island. Their journey proved that Tasmania was an island. This was an important discovery because it meant ships sailing to or from England could save time by sailing through Bass Strait instead of around the bottom of Tasmania.

Between 1802 and 1803 Flinders circumnavigated Australia on the *Investigator*. His charts of the coastline were very accurate and used by sailors for many years.

**Circumnavigate* means 'travel all the way around'.

1. *Robinson Crusoe* is
   - **A** a boat.
   - **B** an adventure story.
   - **C** a real person.
   - **D** a place in England.

2. When did the HMS *Reliance*, with Bass and Flinders aboard, arrive in Sydney?
   - **A** 1796
   - **B** 1678
   - **C** 1795
   - **D** 1798

3. Who built the *Norfolk*?
   - **A** Bass
   - **B** Flinders
   - **C** convicts
   - **D** Tom Thumb

4. During 1802 and 1803 Flinders circumnavigated
   - **A** Australia.
   - **B** the George's River.
   - **C** London.
   - **D** Van Diemen's Land.

5. Why was it important to discover if Tasmania was an island?

   ....

   ....

   ....

   ....

   ....

Answers and explanations on p. 95

Fact-finding questions

Use the **Step-by-step guide** on pages 24–27 to help you read the text and **find facts** to answer the questions below. Circle the correct answers or write your answer on the lines.

How to throw a boomerang

A boomerang is a curved piece of material, usually wood, that returns to you if you throw it in the correct way. Boomerangs were first used by Indigenous Australians as hunting weapons and for ceremonial purposes. Learning to throw and catch a boomerang takes plenty of practice.

What you need:

- a lightweight boomerang with a wing design that allows it to return
- plenty of space so you are not too close to other people or to places where your boomerang can get trapped
- a calm day with no more than a moderate wind.

Method:

1. Hold the boomerang at the end with its V point or elbow pointing towards you. The flat side should be against the palm of your hand.
2. Stand at a slight angle so the wind is coming towards your left cheek.
3. Lift the boomerang up straight and adjust to the angle of 1 o'clock.
4. Step forward and bend your arm back to throw the boomerang as though you are casting a fishing line. Given enough force this will enable it to spin.
5. Don't take your eyes off the boomerang. That way you can be in place to catch it when it returns.

1 What is a boomerang usually made from?

A plastic
B wood
C stone
D fabric

2 The boomerang's V point is also called

A its wing.
B its curved side.
C its elbow.
D its end.

3 Where do you place the palm of your hand on a boomerang before you throw it?

A on the elbow
B against its flat side
C against its curved side
D in its middle

4 You should throw the boomerang

A like a tennis ball.
B where it can be trapped.
C directly into the wind.
D like casting a fishing line.

5 Why should you keep your eyes on the boomerang? Explain your answer.

....

....

....

....

....

Answers and explanations on pp. 95–96

Step-by-step guide to **synthesis** questions

Synthesis questions involve connecting ideas and information from across the text.

Use this **Step-by-step guide** to help you read the text and **synthesise** information to answer the questions below. Circle the correct answers or write your answer on the lines.

STEP 1 **Skim** the text to see what it is about and how it is organised.	**Read** the title, *Sea Turtles*. Look at the illustration and other visual elements. Notice what the picture of the sea turtle tells you about these creatures. Notice the layout of the text in paragraphs. Make **predictions** about its subject and purpose.
STEP 2 **Read** the text. **Monitor** your reading to make sure you understand the text.	**Visualise** and **connect** with the ideas in the text**. Think** about what you already know about the subject and the type of text, a report. Make **predictions.** Make **inferences**. Reflect on meanings and make **judgements**.

Sea turtles

When nesting, the female sea turtle uses her flippers and rotates her body to make a hole deep in the sand. She lays a hundred or more eggs at the bottom, packs the sand back, then returns to the sea. Some nests are dug up by animals or poachers.

After hatching eight weeks later, the baby sea turtles burrow their way up through the sand. This short journey can take up to a week. When the baby sea turtles emerge, they are about 4.5 centimetres long. Then begins their journey to the sea. Predators, dehydration in the sun, waves sweeping them back to shore and other dangers mean many never make the open ocean. At best, only one in 1000 will survive.

The open ocean has its own dangers for sea turtles. Sea creatures and birds eat them. Nets, line hooks and boat propellers unintentionally trap them. They are still hunted by humans even though many species are endangered.

Those who survive migrate hundreds of miles. In the nesting season the female often returns to the nesting beach and lays her eggs close to where she first hatched. Sea turtles have behaved in this way since the time of the dinosaurs.

Question 1 **Sea turtle eggs are soft-shelled and papery to leathery in texture. To which paragraph could this information be added?**

A paragraph one B paragraph two C paragraph three D paragraph four

STEP 3 **Read** the question. **Think** about what type of question it is. Work out what you need to do to answer it.	This is a **synthesis** question. **Think** about which paragraphs refer to sea turtle eggs.

STEP 4 Remember what you have read and **visualised**. **Think** about how ideas in the text relate to each other.

Think about the paragraphs that refer to sea turtle eggs. To answer the question you need to select the paragraph where this information is most relevant.

A is correct. This is a **synthesis** question. The first paragraph is mainly about how sea turtles lay eggs and what can happen to those eggs before they hatch. The sentence 'Sea turtle eggs are soft-shelled and papery to leathery in texture' gives more information about the eggs and helps explain how it is easy for predators to harm them.

Check the other options to confirm why they are incorrect. **B** and **C** are incorrect as these paragraphs are not about the eggs of baby sea turtles. **D** is incorrect because paragraph four mentions eggs in relation to the behaviour of sea turtles. The information about the texture of the eggs is not relevant to this.

Question 2 Which two paragraphs are mostly about adult sea turtle behaviour?

A paragraphs one and two

B paragraphs two and three

C paragraphs three and four

D paragraphs one and four

STEP 3 **Read** the question. **Think** about what type of question it is. Work out what you need to do to answer it.

This is a **synthesis** question. **Think** about what each paragraph is mostly about.

STEP 4 Remember what you have read and **visualised**. **Think** about how ideas in the text relate to each other.

Scan the text for references to adult sea turtles. Re-read these parts to check if they are about the way adult turtles behave.

D is correct. This is a **synthesis** question. The first paragraph gives information about adult female sea turtles when nesting. Paragraph four gives information about adult sea turtles' migratory habits and where they nest.

Check the other options to confirm why they are incorrect. Neither paragraphs two nor three refer to adult sea turtles or their behaviour so **B** and **C** are incorrect.

Question 3 Which sentence has information relevant mainly to the last paragraph?

A Sea turtles' shells vary in colour.

B Females nest only at night and at high tide.

C Some species of sea turtles journey thousands of miles.

D Most male sea turtles have enlarged claws on their front flippers.

STEP 3 **Read** the question. **Think** about what type of question it is. Work out what you need to do to answer it.

This is a **synthesis** question. **Think** about what the last paragraph is mainly about.

STEP 4 Remember what you have read and **visualised**. **Think** about how ideas in the text relate to each other.

Check each sentence to see if it has any relevance to what the last paragraph is mainly about.

C is correct. This is a **synthesis** question. The last paragraph is mainly about the kind of journeys sea turtles have taken since the time of the dinosaurs. The sentence 'Some species of sea turtles journey thousands of miles' adds relevant information to this topic.

Check the other options to confirm why they are incorrect. **A**, **B** and **D** are incorrect as the information in these sentences is not about the journeys turtles make.

Step-by-step guide to **synthesis** questions *continued*

Synthesis questions involve connecting ideas and information from across the text.

Sea turtles

When nesting, the female sea turtle uses her flippers and rotates her body to make a hole deep in the sand. She lays a hundred or more eggs at the bottom, packs the sand back, then returns to the sea. Some nests are dug up by animals or poachers.

After hatching eight weeks later, the baby sea turtles burrow their way up through the sand. This short journey can take up to a week. When the baby sea turtles emerge, they are about 4.5 centimetres long. Then begins their journey to the sea. Predators, dehydration in the sun, waves sweeping them back to shore and other dangers mean many never make the open ocean. At best, only one in 1000 will survive.

The open ocean has its own dangers for sea turtles. Sea creatures and birds eat them. Nets, line hooks and boat propellers unintentionally trap them. They are still hunted by humans even though many species are endangered.

Those who survive migrate hundreds of miles. In the nesting season the female often returns to the nesting beach and lays her eggs close to where she first hatched. Sea turtles have behaved in this way since the time of the dinosaurs.

Question 4 **The main theme running through this text is**

A that some species of sea turtles are endangered.
B that being a sea turtle has many dangers.
C that there are gender differences in sea turtle behaviour.
D the migratory habits of the sea turtle.

STEP 3 **Read** the question. **Think** about what type of question it is. Work out what you need to do to answer it.

- This is a **synthesis** question. **Think** about any themes that run through the text and are important in the text as a whole.

STEP 4 Remember what you have read and **visualised**. **Think** about how ideas in the text relate to each other.

- **Scan** the text for ideas related to each of the themes suggested in the question. Re-read these parts to confirm if the ideas are centrally important in the text.

B is correct. This is a **synthesis** question. Each paragraph, except for the last, includes information about dangers faced by sea turtles. This is an important idea in the text.

Check the other options to confirm why they are incorrect. **A** is incorrect because although it is said that some species of sea turtle are endangered, this is not a theme of the whole text. **C** is incorrect because gender differences in sea turtle behaviour are touched on in paragraphs one and four but are not a theme of the text as a whole. **D** is incorrect as the migratory habits of sea turtles are only referred to in paragraph four.

Question 5 Which statement is NOT true of sea turtles?

A Most baby sea turtles survive.
B Most baby sea turtles fail to survive.
C Baby sea turtles hatch from eggs.
D Adult sea turtles have flippers and shells.

STEP 3 **Read** the question. **Think** about what type of question it is. Work out what you need to do to answer it.

- This is a **synthesis** question. You need to work out which of the given statements is NOT true of sea turtles.

STEP 4 Remember what you have read and **visualised**. **Think** about how ideas in the text relate to each other.

- **Re-read** the text. Check the statements to see if their information is confirmed by the text as true. The statement that is NOT confirmed as being true of sea turtles is the correct answer.

A is correct. This is a **synthesis** question. You read *At best, only one* [baby sea turtle] *in 1000 will survive (see line 14).* This means most baby sea turtles fail to survive. This makes **A** the statement that is NOT true.

Check the other options to confirm why they are incorrect. **B** is incorrect because it is true that most baby sea turtles fail to survive. **C** is incorrect because it is a true statement. You read *She lays a hundred or more eggs in a nest … After hatching eight weeks later, the baby sea turtles … (see lines 4 and 8–9).* This means that baby sea turtles hatch from eggs. **D** is incorrect because it is true that adult sea turtles have both flippers and shells. They are referred to in the text (flippers in paragraph one; shells in paragraph three) and in the illustration.

Question 6 In what ways do humans harm sea turtles?

Explain your answer on the lines below.

STEP 3 **Read** the question. **Think** about what type of question it is. Work out what you need to do to answer it.

- This is a **synthesis** question. You need to **work out** what humans do that causes harm to sea turtles.

STEP 4 Remember what you have read and **visualised**. **Think** about how ideas in the text relate to each other.

- **Scan** the text for references to humans and sea turtles. Re-read each of these parts and decide if they describe ways that humans cause harm to sea turtles.

You read *Some nests are dug up by animals or poachers (see lines 6–7)* and *Nets, line hooks and boat propellors unintentionally trap them (see lines 15–16).* They have been hunted by humans for food and their shells are also prized. This means humans steal the eggs of sea turtles, endanger the turtles with their fishing methods and hunt them for food and their shells.

Synthesis questions

Use the **Step-by-step guide** on pages 32–35 to help you read the text and **synthesise** information to answer the questions below. Circle the correct answers or write your answer on the lines.

How to make Anzac biscuits

These biscuits were originally made to send to ANZAC soldiers fighting in the First World War. You will notice the recipe doesn't have any eggs. This is because there was a scarcity of eggs during the war when many poultry farmers left their farms to join the armed forces. The biscuits also keep longer without eggs.

To make them, you need:

- 1 cup flour, sifted
- 1 cup caster sugar
- 1 cup coconut
- 2 cups rolled oats or wheat bran
- 125 g unsalted butter
- 2 tbsp golden syrup
- 1 tsp bicarbonate soda
- 3 tbsp boiling water

Method

1. Heat oven to 180 °C (160 °C fan bake). Place baking paper on baking trays. Combine flour, caster sugar, coconut and oats in a bowl and stir with a wooden spoon. Make a well in the centre of this mixture.
2. Place butter and golden syrup in a saucepan to melt. Dissolve baking soda in boiling water. Pour these ingredients into the well and mix together.
3. Roll spoonfuls of the mixture into balls and press onto baking trays, leaving space between them.
4. Bake for 15 minutes until golden brown. Place on a wire rack to cool.

1 Paragraph one is different from the rest of the text because

A it is the shortest paragraph.

B it tells you what to do first.

C it gives background information.

D it tells you how to make the biscuits.

2 The dot points list

A ingredients.

B dry ingredients.

C wet ingredients.

D utensils.

3 What extra information would be helpful for making ANZAC biscuits?

A information about ANZAC Day

B information about how to keep your oven clean

C a list of the utensils you will use

D a list of different types of biscuits you could cook

4 Which information is NOT included in this text?

A Eggs are not used to make these biscuits.

B These biscuits were sent to ANZAC soldiers.

C Either wheat bran or rolled oats can be used.

D The recipe makes about 30 biscuits.

5 To which part of the text could you add this sentence?

Add choc chips to the mixture to make a different kind of biscuit.

Explain your reasons.

....

....

....

Answers and explanations on p. 96

Synthesis questions

Use the **Step-by-step guide** on pages 32–35 to help you read the text and **synthesise** information to answer the questions below. Circle the correct answers or write your answer on the lines.

Can I have a worm farm, please?

Marietta: Mum, can I have a worm farm, please?

Mum: They're too expensive, Marietta. Why do you want one anyway?

Marietta: I'm interested in worms. And we've been learning about composting at school. It's really important to save waste. You can feed the worms all our kitchen scraps. They chomp through them and they make liquid fertiliser to use on our vegetables.

Mum: I can see it's a good idea but …

Marietta: It's a really good idea, Mum. Your vegetables will grow better and think how much rubbish won't have to be collected and how much landfill won't be used. It mounts up over time.

Mum: Yes, good point. But you can't get around the expense, Marietta.

Marietta: I think you can, Mum. What I want is to make the farm out of foam boxes that you can get free from our fruit shop. I've read the instructions on the internet and I know I can do it. You'd only need to pay for the worms and a plastic tap to add to a box to let the liquid out.

Mum: Where would I get the worms?

Marietta: Worm farms or at a garden nursery. Perleeeze, Mum.

Mum: You *have* done your research well, Marietta. OK then. You can have your worm farm.

1. What does Marietta want to persuade her mum to do?
   - **A** buy her a worm farm
   - **B** buy her worms and a tap so she can make a worm farm
   - **C** use worm fertiliser on her vegetables
   - **D** learn how to compost waste

2. Which is NOT an argument Marietta uses for having a worm farm?
   - **A** You get fertiliser you can use on your vegetables.
   - **B** You help save waste going in to landfill.
   - **C** You get free vegetables.
   - **D** You have less rubbish to get rid of.

3. What solution does Marietta have for worm farms being expensive?
   - **A** She can make her own worm farm very cheaply.
   - **B** She can save up her pocket money.
   - **C** Her mum will save money as she won't have to buy fertiliser.
   - **D** She can bottle and label the fertiliser and sell it to friends.

4. What other points could Marietta have added to support her request? Choose all that apply.
   - **A** It is well known that reducing landfill reduces harmful greenhouse gases.
   - **B** It is usually not a good idea to transfer compost worms to garden soil.
   - **C** Everyone in the class has a worm farm.
   - **D** Worm farms are easy to look after as they do most of the work.

5. What finally persuades Marietta's mother to agree to Marietta's request?

   ....

   ....

Answers and explanations on pp. 96–97

Synthesis questions

Use the **Step-by-step guide** on pages 32–35 to help you read the text and **synthesise** information to answer the questions below. Circle the correct answers or write your answer on the lines.

Doctor Dolittle

'Do you think I would ever be able to learn the language of the animals?' [asked Tommy Stubbins] …

'Well, it all depends,' said Polynesia. 'Are you clever at lessons?'

'I don't know,' I answered, feeling rather ashamed. 'You see, I've never been to school. My father is too poor to send me.'

'Well,' said the parrot, 'I don't suppose you have really missed much—to judge from what I have seen of school-boys. But listen: are you a good noticer? Do you notice things well? I mean, for instance, supposing you saw two cock-starlings on an apple-tree, and you only took one good look at them—would you be able to tell one from the other if you saw them again the next day?'

'I don't know,' I said. 'I've never tried.'

'Well that,' said Polynesia, brushing some crumbs off the corner of the table with her left foot 'that is what you call powers of observation—noticing the small things about birds and animals: the way they walk and move their heads and flip their wings; the way they sniff the air and twitch their whiskers and wiggle their tails. You have to notice all those little things if you want to learn animal language.'

Extract from *The Voyages of Doctor Dolittle* by Hugh Lofting, 1922

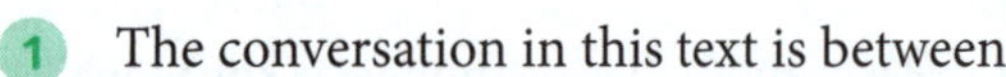

1. The conversation in this text is between
   - **A** Polynesia and Tommy Stubbins's father.
   - **B** Tommy Stubbins and Polynesia.
   - **C** Doctor Dolittle and Tommy Stubbins.
   - **D** Polynesia and Doctor Dolittle.

2. The conversation in the text is mainly about
   - **A** whether Tommy Stubbins will be able to learn animal language.
   - **B** how clever Tommy Stubbins is.
   - **C** the powers of observation.
   - **D** whether Polynesia can teach Tommy Stubbins animal language.

3. Which of these does Polynesia think is the least important when learning animal language?
   - **A** noticing
   - **B** comparing
   - **C** being clever at lessons
   - **D** observing

3. Which information is NOT included in the text? Choose all that apply.
   - **A** details about what made Tommy's family poor
   - **B** details about Doctor Dolittle's voyages
   - **C** details about Polynesia's family background
   - **D** details about powers of observation

5. What is the main thing Polynesia thinks you have to do to learn animal language?

....

....

....

....

....

Answers and explanations on p. 97

Synthesis questions

Use the **Step-by-step guide** on pages 32–35 to help you read the text and **synthesise** information to answer the questions below. Circle the correct answers or write your answer on the lines.

Bunyips

The bunyip is part of Australian folklore. First Nations mythology tells of the bunyip as a spirit found in creeks, rivers, swamps and billabongs. Some Dreamtime stories show the bunyip as an evil, punishing spirit. Other tales present it as a creature which frightens people because of its appearance but, in itself, is shy and rather lonely.

There have been many sightings of bunyips reported in Australia in the past. In 1846 something that looked like a large platypus sunning itself on the banks of the Yarra River was thought to be a bunyip. Some men in a boat planned to catch it, but it disappeared when they were only a metre away. Then in 1847, what was thought to be a bunyip's skull was put on display at the Australian Museum. No-one was able to prove it came from a bunyip because it mysteriously disappeared from the display.

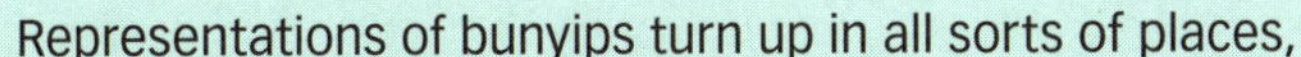

Representations of bunyips turn up in all sorts of places, such as pantomimes, picture books, poems and songs. In 1994 a bunyip appeared on Australian postage stamps! No two bunyips ever seem to look the same though they are often hairy and large, have red eyes, trail weeds and have a terrifying cry.

1. The main purpose of this text is to
   - **A** discuss Australian folklore.
   - **B** report on the bunyip's role in Australian folklore.
   - **C** describe bunyips.
   - **D** report on a Dreamtime story.
2. Paragraph two is about
   - **A** possible evidence of bunyips' existence.
   - **B** bunyips' adventures.
   - **C** what bunyips look like.
   - **D** the bunyip's habits.
3. Which of the following records the bunyip's most recent appearance?
   - **A** a 'bunyip' sighting on the Yarra River
   - **B** the display of a 'bunyip' skull in the Australian Museum
   - **C** Dreamtime stories about the bunyip
   - **D** the appearance of the bunyip on postage stamps
4. What is NOT true of bunyips?
   - **A** They are thought of as something to be feared.
   - **B** Their existence has been proved scientifically.
   - **C** Their existence has not yet been proved scientifically.
   - **D** There have been sightings of them reported.
5. What would you expect a bunyip to look like? Explain the reasons for your answer.

Answers and explanations on pp. 97–98

Step-by-step guide to **inferring** questions

Inferring questions involve reading between the lines to work out an answer that is not stated directly in the text.

Use this **Step-by-step guide** to help you read the text and make **inferences** to answer the questions below. Circle the correct answers or write your answer on the lines.

STEP 1	**Skim** the text to see what it is about and how it is organised.	**Read** the title, *Gulliver's Travels*. Look at the illustrations and other visual elements. Notice the picture of Gulliver pegged to the ground with little creatures swarming all over him and **predict** what it suggests has happened. Notice the text is one long paragraph. Make **predictions** about the type and purpose of the text.
STEP 2	**Read** the text. **Monitor** your reading to make sure you understand the text.	**Visualise** and **connect** with the ideas in the text. **Think** about what you already know about the type of text, a narrative. Notice that the information at the end of the text says it is an extract from *Gulliver's Travels*, which means it is part of a larger narrative. Make **predictions.** Make **inferences**. Reflect on meanings and make **judgements**.

Gulliver's Travels

I [Gulliver] lay down on the grass, which was very short and soft, where I slept sounder than ever I remembered to have done in my life, and, as I reckoned, about nine hours; for when I awaked, it was just day-light. I attempted to rise, but was not able to stir: for, as I happened to lie on my back, I found my arms and legs were strongly fastened on each side to the ground; and my hair, which was long and thick, tied down in the same manner ... I heard a confused noise about me; but in the posture I lay, could see nothing except the sky. In a little time I felt something alive moving on my left leg, which advancing gently forward over my breast, came almost up to my chin; when, bending my eyes downwards as much as I could, I perceived it to be a human creature not six inches high [15 centimetres], with a bow and arrow in his hands, and a quiver at his back. In the mean time, I felt at least forty more of the same kind ... I was in the utmost astonishment, and roared so loud, that they all ran back in a fright; and some of them, as I was afterwards told, were hurt with the falls they got by leaping from my sides upon the ground.

Extract from *Gulliver's Travels* by Jonathan Swift, 1726

Question 1 What happened to Gulliver while he was asleep?

A He dreamed a strange dream.
B He was tied down to the ground.
C He began to snore.
D He leaped up.

STEP (3)	**Read** the question. **Think** about what type of question it is. Work out what you need to do to answer it.	This is an **inferring** question. The answer is not stated directly in the text. You need to work out what happened to Gulliver while he was asleep.
STEP (4)	**Think** about the text. Remember what you have read and **visualised**.	**Scan** the text to find the part when he wakes up. Work out what is inferred about what has happened to him.

B is correct. This is an **inferring** question. You can **infer** that when Gulliver was asleep his arms, legs and hair were tied to the ground so he couldn't move.

Check the other options to confirm why they are incorrect. **A**, **C** and **D** are incorrect as there is no evidence in the text to suggest that when he was asleep he dreamed (**A**), snored (**C**) or leaped up (**D**).

Question 2 Why could he only see the sky?

A He was on his back.
B He couldn't open his eyes properly.
C There was nothing else to see.
D He was on his back and had his hair tied to the ground.

STEP (3)	**Read** the question. **Think** about what type of question it is. Work out what you need to do to answer it.	This is an **inferring** question. The answer is not stated directly in the text. You need to read between the lines and work out why Gulliver could only see the sky.
STEP (4)	Remember what you have read and **visualised**.	Re-read what is said about how Gulliver is lying on the ground. Look at the illustration and **visualise** what you could see from Gulliver's position to **infer** what could explain why Gulliver can only see the sky.

D is correct. This is an **inferring** question. Gulliver is lying on his back and his hair is tied down. You can **infer** that this would stop him moving his head from side to side. This means all he would be able to see when his eyes are open is what is above him—the sky.

Check the other options to confirm why they are incorrect. **A** is incorrect because it is not just being on his back; it is also having his hair tied down to stop his head from moving. **B** is incorrect as there is no evidence that he can't open his eyes. **C** is incorrect because there are other things to see around him.

Question 3 What made the confused noise that Gulliver heard?

A something alive on his leg
B bows and arrows being put back
C forty human creatures moving about
D the voices of other people

STEP (3)	**Read** the question. **Think** about what type of question it is. Work out what you need to do to answer it.	This is an **inferring** question. The answer is not stated directly in the text. You need to read between the lines and work out what made the confused noise heard by Gulliver.
STEP (4)	Remember what you have read and **visualised**.	Re-read the part about what is happening to Gulliver to **infer** who is there and what is causing the confused noise that is made.

C is correct. This is an **inferring** question. You can **infer** that the confused noise Gulliver hears is made by forty human creatures moving about his body. There is no-one else mentioned in the text who is making a noise.

Check the other options to confirm why they are incorrect. **A** is incorrect because something alive on his leg is only part of what makes the confused noise. **B** is incorrect because we are not told that the bows and arrows are put back. **D** is incorrect because you cannot infer that the confused noise Gulliver hears is made by voices of other people speaking, since no-one else seems to be there.

Step-by-step guide to **inferring** questions *continued*

Inferring questions involve reading between the lines to work out an answer that is not stated directly in the text.

Gulliver's Travels

I [Gulliver] lay down on the grass, which was very short and soft, where I slept sounder than ever I remembered to have done in my life, and, as I reckoned, about nine hours; for when I awaked, it was just day-light. I attempted to rise, but was not able to stir: for, as I happened to lie on my back, I found my arms and legs were strongly fastened on each side to the ground; and my hair, which was long and thick, tied down in the same manner ... I heard a confused noise about me; but in the posture I lay, could see nothing except the sky. In a little time I felt something alive moving on my left leg, which advancing gently forward over my breast, came almost up to my chin; when, bending my eyes downwards as much as I could, I perceived it to be a human creature not six inches high [15 centimetres], with a bow and arrow in his hands, and a quiver at his back. In the mean time, I felt at least forty more of the same kind ... I was in the utmost astonishment, and roared so loud, that they all ran back in a fright; and some of them, as I was afterwards told, were hurt with the falls they got by leaping from my sides upon the ground.

Extract from *Gulliver's Travels* by Jonathan Swift, 1726

Question 4 **Gulliver's roar of astonishment is caused by his realisation that**

A a bow and arrow is about to be fired at him.
B a little human creature is moving close to his chin.
C there are at least 40 tiny human creatures with bows and arrows on his body.
D his hair is tied to the ground so he cannot move.

STEP 3 **Read** the question. **Think** about what type of question it is. Work out what you need to do to answer it.

- This is an **inferring** question. The answer is not stated directly in the text. You need to read between the lines and work out the cause of Gulliver's astonishment.

STEP 4 Remember what you have read and **visualised**.

- Re-read the text to work out what is the main cause of Gulliver roaring in astonishment. **Think** about all the things that might cause Gulliver to express his astonishment and which of these triggers his cry.

C is correct. This is an **inferring** question. Gulliver's roar of astonishment comes when he realizes that the movements over his body are caused by forty or so tiny human creatures with bows and arrows.

Check the other options to confirm why they are incorrect. **A** is incorrect because, although realising he is in danger from a bow and arrow is surprising to Gulliver, this is not what causes him to roar with astonishment. **B** is incorrect because, while he is surprised to see a little creature with a bow and arrow near his chin, it is learning that there are forty more of these creatures that causes him to roar. **D** is incorrect because, although you assume that Gulliver is surprised to find himself unable to move his head, this is not what causes him to roar.

Question 5 Why would the human creatures be hurt by falling from Gulliver?

Explain your answer on the lines below.

STEP 3 **Read** the question. **Think** about what type of question it is. Work out what you need to do to answer it.

- This is an **inferring** question. The answer is not stated directly in the text. You need to work out why some creatures would hurt themselves when they leaped or fell from Gulliver's body.

STEP 4 Remember what you have read and **visualised**.

- **Scan** the text to find information about the size of the creatures. Look at the illustration to compare the size of the creatures with that of Gulliver's size; then **infer** the distance from Gulliver to the ground from the point of view of the creatures.

This is an **inferring** question. Your answer needs to explain the creatures, who were less than 15 centimetres high and quite some distance from the ground when they were standing on Gulliver. The ladders in the illustration show that they needed help to get up on to Gulliver's body. This means it is likely some of them would be hurt when they leaped or fell from his body.

Question 6 Had Gulliver visited this place on his travels before?

Explain your answer on the lines below.

STEP 3 **Read** the question. **Think** about what type of question it is. Work out what you need to do to answer it.

- This is an **inferring** question. The answer is not stated directly in the text. You need to work out whether or not there is evidence to show that Gulliver had visited this place before.

STEP 4 **Remember** what you have read and **visualised**.

- **Scan** the text to find information about what Gulliver knows about the place and its people. **Think** about what you can **infer** from his actions.

This is an **inferring** question. Your answer needs to explain that there is no evidence Gulliver has been to this place before. When he arrives he sleeps on the grass. This suggests he knows nothing of the danger he is placing himself in. He is also astonished by the sight of the people who live there. It is clear he has never seen them before.

Inferring questions

Use the **Step-by-step guide** on pages 40–43 to help you read the text and make **inferences** to answer the questions below. Circle the correct answers or write your answer on the lines.

Tell me about Tokyo

New | Reply | Delete | Archive | Junk | Sweep | Move to

To: Akihito@Tokyosisterschool.com

Hi Akihito

I am pleased that my teacher has arranged for you to be my email buddy.

I live on Kangaroo Island, a small island off South Australia. I live in a big house overlooking the ocean and we keep bees in our garden. My brother and I ride our bikes to school. At weekends I love to go fishing. Our long school holiday is in January when it gets very hot. When we go to the mainland we have to put our car on the ferry.

Please tell me about your life in Tokyo.

Elly

New | Reply | Delete | Archive | Junk | Sweep | Move to

To: Elly@KIsisterschool.com

Hi Elly

Your life sounds different from mine. Tokyo is a very busy capital city with more than 13 million people living here, including me :) Everything is open 24/7 and trains take you everywhere you want to go. I live in a small apartment with my parents and sister.

We don't have a car. I walk to school. Our custom is not to wear our outdoor shoes inside our homes or our classrooms so I take them off when I arrive. We often have earthquake drills as Tokyo is on the Ring of Fire. Our long holiday is in July.

At weekends I like taking purikuras (instant photos). I'm attaching a photo of Mount Fuji for you.

Akihito

 Mount Fuji

1. An email buddy is a person with whom you exchange messages
   - **A** using a pen.
   - **B** using an electronic device such as an iPad or laptop.
   - **C** using the telephone.
   - **D** using the post.

2. Elly's life is different from Akihito's life because
   - **A** she is an only child.
   - **B** she goes to school.
   - **C** she lives with her family.
   - **D** she lives on a small island off the mainland.

3. Why is Akihito's life different from Elly's? Choose all that apply.
   - **A** His long school holidays are in July.
   - **B** He has earthquake drills at school.
   - **C** His hobby is photography.
   - **D** He lives in a small apartment.

4. Why does Akihito's family not have a car? Choose all that apply.
   - **A** They can't afford one.
   - **B** The train service is very good.
   - **C** The streets are very crowded.
   - **D** It was towed away.

5. What Japanese tradition does Akihito always follow?

   ....

   ....

   ....

   ....

Answers and explanations on p. 98

Inferring questions

Use the **Step-by-step guide** on pages 40–43 to help you read the text and make **inferences** to answer the questions below. Circle the correct answers or write your answer on the lines.

How the birds got their colours

One day, Dove was searching for seeds when she stabbed her foot on the prong of a tree root. It hurt. It bled.

'Help,' she cooed. 'Help me.'

The bird tribes heard her cry and flocked to where she lay on the ground. A cloak of black birds gathered around her. (The birds were black because back in the Dreamtime all birds in the bird tribes were black.) They could see her foot was swollen and painful.

'I'll get water,' cried Duck.

'I'll bathe your wound,' called Kingfisher.

Crow glowered darkly at Dove. He didn't like everyone fussing around her instead of paying attention to him.

'Leave her. You're wasting your time,' croaked Crow.

'Get lost Crow,' called the other birds. Together they chased him away.

The swelling on Dove's foot was getting worse, not better.

'I have an idea,' cried Galah. Swooping at Dove's foot, she pierced the swelling with her hooked beak. At once all the colours of the rainbow burst from it, splashing and spattering the birds. Magpie got just a splash of white; others like Lorikeet were covered with many bright colours. Dove's colour drained away, leaving her pale and softly mottled.

So that is how the birds got their colours. Only Crow missed out. Crow has stayed black to this day.

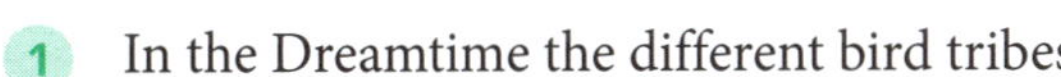

1 In the Dreamtime the different bird tribes
- **A** were unkind to each other.
- **B** took care of each other.
- **C** ignored each other.
- **D** spread rumours about each other.

2 Why did Crow glower darkly at Dove?
- **A** He'd never liked her.
- **B** He could see she was going to die.
- **C** He was jealous of all the attention she was getting.
- **D** He was nasty to everyone.

3 Who was mainly responsible for saving Dove's life?
- **A** Galah
- **B** Crow
- **C** Duck
- **D** Kingfisher

4 Dove's feathers became
- **A** rainbow coloured.
- **B** blacker than ever.
- **C** splashed with white.
- **D** faded and light in colour.

5 Why has Crow stayed black to this day?

....

....

....

....

....

Answers and explanations on pp. 98–99

Inferring questions

Use the **Step-by-step guide** on pages 40–43 to help you read the text and make **inferences** to answer the questions below. Circle the correct answers or write your answer on the lines.

Should school uniforms be compulsory?

Harry: I don't think uniforms should be compulsory. Uniforms make everyone look the same.

Mina: But that can be a good thing. Sporting teams wear uniforms and have mascots and things. Wearing a uniform connects you with the other students. It builds your school spirit.

Jack: You don't need a uniform to build school spirit.

Mina: Of course not. But if there's a good spirit then it's a good feeling to be in your uniform.

Carey: And it's so easy putting on a uniform. You don't even have to think.

Peta: My friend goes to a school where they don't wear uniforms. She says you don't think about it after the first few days.

Jack: What's the point of them though? Why should we have to wear them if we don't want to?

Mina: It's a way of identifying a group. When you're at a sporting carnival or on an excursion, for example.

Harry: Wearing a uniform makes me feel locked up inside so I can't be me.

Mina: It's not that bad! We should have a choice then. There'd be school uniforms but no-one would have to wear them. I think that would work.

Peta: Perhaps that is a good way forward. Let's go with that view.

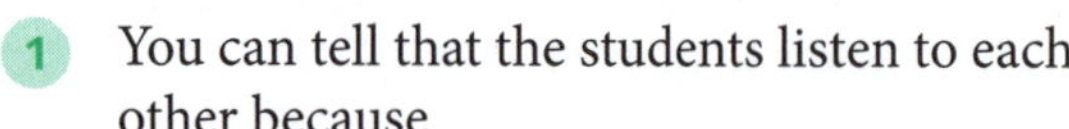

1. You can tell that the students listen to each other because
   - **A** they express different opinions.
   - **B** they comment on each other's ideas.
   - **C** they always disagree with what has just been said.
   - **D** they act politely.

2. Who supports the view that school uniforms should NOT be compulsory? Choose all that apply.
   - **A** Harry
   - **B** Peta
   - **C** Jack
   - **D** Carey

3. Whose point of view changes during the discussion?
   - **A** Harry's
   - **B** Mina's
   - **C** Jack's
   - **D** Carey's

4. Peta reports on her friend's experience to
   - **A** explain that wearing everyday clothes needn't be a problem.
   - **B** show she has friends outside this group.
   - **C** point out that Carey is completely mistaken.
   - **D** suggest she is wiser than everybody else.

5. Why does Peta say *Perhaps that is a good way forward* (line 24)?

....

....

....

....

Answers and explanations on p. 99

Inferring questions

Use the **Step-by-step guide** on pages 40–43 to help you read the text and make **inferences** to answer the questions below. Circle the correct answers or write your answer on the lines.

Whodunnit?

(morning)

Thomas: Last night someone put small holes and little piles of earth all over our lawn.

Izzy: Martians perhaps?

Thomas: Yes, for sure!

Izzy: Maybe it was Woof?

Thomas: Doubt it. His paws are too wide to make these little holes. So's his nose.

Izzy: Something with a long thin nose then?

Thomas: Maybe a bird's beak?

Izzy: A kookaburra perhaps? But they usually just swoop to get worms and then fly off. They don't burrow.

Thomas: Mmmm. I'm going to Google it.

(afternoon)

Izzy: What did you find out?

Thomas: Could be bandicoots.

Izzy: I thought they were mythical creatures.

Thomas: That's bunyips. A bandicoot is like a big mouse with sharp claws and a long pointed nose that it uses to forage for food. They sleep in the day and search for food at night.

Izzy: Could be them then. Let's ask Mum and Dad if we can sleep in the tent tonight and keep watch. We'll take turns.

(next morning)

Izzy: *(yawning)* Did you see any bandicoots?

Thomas: Nup. And you slept right through your turn, Izzy.

Izzy: Did not.

Thomas: Something's been here again. Look. More earthcastles!

Izzy: Invisible Martians?

Thomas: Nup, invisible bandicoots. Has to be!

1 Who or what is Woof?

- **A** their giraffe
- **B** their baby brother
- **C** their budgerigar
- **D** their dog

2 When Thomas says *Yes, for sure!* (line 7) to Izzy he implies that

- **A** he thinks she's certainly right.
- **B** he likes her explanation.
- **C** he knows this is not the explanation.
- **D** he thinks she might be right.

3 Why are bandicoots likely suspects for putting holes in the lawn? Choose all that apply.

- **A** They have sharp claws.
- **B** They forage for food in the night.
- **C** They are like big mice.
- **D** They have long pointy noses.

4 Why didn't Thomas or Izzy see the bandicoots?

- **A** The bandicoots were invisible.
- **B** They were probably asleep when the bandicoots visited.
- **C** There weren't any bandicoots.
- **D** Invisible Martians caused the holes.

5 What relation are Thomas and Izzy to each other?

....

....

....

....

Answers and explanations on pp. 99–100

Inferring questions

Use the **Step-by-step guide** on pages 40–43 to help you read the text and make **inferences** to answer the questions below. Circle the correct answers or write your answer on the lines.

Which did you choose?

Inari: We had to name our favourite picture book in class today.

Pablo: So did we. It took me ages to think of one. I read chapter books all the time now.

Inari: Mr Copper said he's making a display of Year Three's favourite picture books in the library for Book Week. Which did you choose?

Pablo: *The Two Bullies* by Junko Morimoto. Have you read that?

Inari: Yes. Such big scary men and yet they end up not fighting! It makes you laugh. That illustration of Ni-ou crossing the Pacific Ocean to reach China is great.

Pablo: Yes, its illustrations are what make it special. Which did you choose?

Inari: Well, I chose *The Red Tree* by Shaun Tan for the same reason as you. It's the illustrations that make it so amazing.

Pablo: I'm not really that interested in red trees.

Inari: Duh! It isn't about red trees. It's about when things go wrong and get worse and worse and nobody understands. The last picture is … oh, but I'll spoil it if I tell you.

Pablo: Wait. I remember now. Shaun Tan made that awesome movie called *The Lost Thing*, didn't he? I think I will give your red tree book a try.

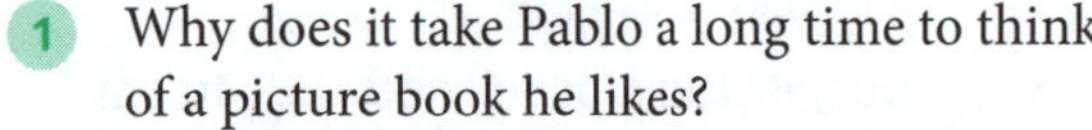

1. Why does it take Pablo a long time to think of a picture book he likes?
   - **A** He has a very bad memory.
   - **B** He hasn't read any for some time.
   - **C** He has given all his picture books to his little brother.
   - **D** He has never read any picture books.

2. Who is Mr Copper?
   - **A** Inari's father
   - **B** Pablo's father
   - **C** a librarian at the school
   - **D** a policeman

3. Inari thinks *The Two Bullies* is mainly
   - **A** scary.
   - **B** amusing.
   - **C** horrifying.
   - **D** worrying.

4. Why does Pablo think he wouldn't like Inari's choice of picture book? Choose all that apply.
   - **A** He thinks books about red trees would be boring.
   - **B** He knows nothing about red trees.
   - **C** The title doesn't interest him.
   - **D** He dislikes picture books with a lot of words.

5. Why does Pablo change his mind about reading *The Red Tree*?
   - **A** He is interested in Inari's summary of the story.
   - **B** He wants to know what the surprise is in the last picture.
   - **C** He wants to please Inari when he thinks she is disappointed in him.
   - **D** He remembers he really liked another work by the author of *The Red Tree*.

6. What is similar about the way Inari and Pablo make their choices?

   ....

   ....

Answers and explanations on p. 100

Inferring questions

Use the **Step-by-step guide** on pages 40–43 to help you read the text and make **inferences** to answer the questions below. Circle the correct answers or write your answer on the lines.

Harmony Day

Celebrate Australia's cultural diversity at Harmony Day

March 21st from 10 am to 4 pm on the Green

Everyone is welcome.

Everyone Belongs.

1 Wear orange: it represents Harmony Day.

2 Visit the family tree stall. Find out where your ancestors came from.

3 Listen to a thrilling musical act by TheGroup: Japanese flute, Chinese Gu-Zheng, Swiss Hang drum and a didgeridoo.

4 Visit our Art Gallery in a Shed: paintings by children who live in Australia but come from all over the world.

5 Eat a Madly Mixed-up Meal: mezze from the Middle East; pho from Vietnam; mud crab from Sri Lanka; paella from Spain; pavlova from Australia. Just add Arabian coffee or water (from everywhere)!

6 Watch a football match: Irish I-balls v the Ozzie Ostriches (Australian Rules) or Brazilian Nuts v the Dutch Demons (soccer).

7 Enter a competition: Design a Harmony Day LOGO for your school or your community that stands for the idea Everyone Belongs. Great prizes.

8 Make someone new to Australia feel welcome. Invite them to come along to the celebrations with you and your family.

1. Harmony Day celebrates
   - **A** cultural differences.
   - **B** cultural similarities.
   - **C** cultural places.
   - **D** cultural sameness.

2. If you were to design a LOGO for the Harmony Day competition which colour would be a good choice?
   - **A** purple
   - **B** orange
   - **C** blue
   - **D** white

3. What is the main reason TheGroup's musical act is suitable for a Harmony Day celebration?
   - **A** It sounds as if it will be unusual.
   - **B** It says it will be thrilling.
   - **C** People from different cultures will play the instruments.
   - **D** It includes a mix of instruments from different cultures.

4. Which of these Madly Mixed-up Meal offerings is humorously worded?
   - **A** paella from Spain
   - **B** mezze from the Middle East
   - **C** water from everywhere
   - **D** pho from Vietnam

5. What does the *v* (which stands for *versus*) mean in *Irish I-balls v the Ozzie Ostriches* and *Brazilian Nuts v the Dutch Demons*?
   - **A** victory
   - **B** against
   - **C** vote for
   - **D** viewing

6. Which box describes the only thing you can do before attending the Harmony Day celebrations?

   ....

   ....

   ....

Answers and explanations on pp. 100–101

Inferring questions

Use the **Step-by-step guide** on pages 40–43 to help you read the text and make **inferences** to answer the questions below. Circle the correct answers or write your answer on the lines.

Why do birds fly in a V shape?

When birds migrate together they often make a V shape in the sky. Groups of planes also fly in a V formation. It saves on fuel as the planes take advantage of the lift from the movement caused by the plane in front of them. A recent experiment with 14 bald ibises aimed to find out why ibises fly that way. The ibises, raised by human foster parents at a Vienna zoo, were taken on training flights. They were fitted with sensors for their 1000 kilometre migration from Austria to Tuscany. The foster parents rode in a lightweight aircraft attached to a parachute.

It was found that each ibis put itself about 1.2 metres behind the bird in front of it at an angle of about 45 degrees. This was found to be the best position to take advantage of swirls of upward-moving air made by the wings of the bird ahead. They also timed their wing beats carefully to catch the upwash of air.

When the birds changed positions in the V, to give the leader a rest, for example, they changed their wing movements to suit their new position. This removed any doubt about what they were doing. They were conserving their energy on the long flight.

1. How many birds fly at the pointy end of the V shape?
   - **A** one
   - **B** two
   - **C** three
   - **D** four

2. What is the lift made of that helps the planes save fuel?
   - **A** water
   - **B** smoke
   - **C** air
   - **D** rain

3. Why were the ibises fitted with sensors?
   - **A** to send information to the ibises
   - **B** to make the ibises easier to see
   - **C** to record information about the ibises' movements
   - **D** to help the ibises fly further

4. The experiment found that ibises fly in a V shape
   - **A** to keep warm.
   - **B** because they copy the way planes fly.
   - **C** because it feels comfortable for them.
   - **D** to conserve energy on long flights.

5. Does the experiment prove that other long-winged birds such as pelicans, storks and geese know how to save their energy on long flights?

   ....

   ....

   ....

   ....

   ....

Answers and explanations on p. 101

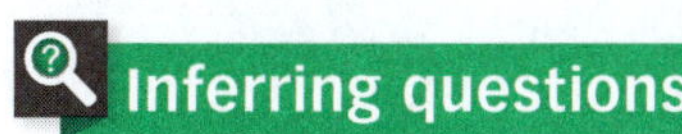

Inferring questions

Use the **Step-by-step guide** on pages 40–43 to help you read the text and make **inferences** to answer the questions below. Circle the correct answers or write your answer on the lines.

How Australia got its name

In Europe, as far back as Roman times, legends told of a land called 'Unknown Land to the South' (*Terra Australis Incognita* in Latin). In fact, First Australians had been living in this 'unknown land' for hundreds of thousands of years.

Later, when European explorers returned with reports of land south of the equator, the name 'Land of the South' (*Terra Australis*) replaced the earlier name. In the 17th century, the Dutch used the name New Holland for areas of Australia that they had charted.

Source: Project Gutenberg

In 1770 Captain Cook claimed the east coast of New Holland for the British government, naming it New South Wales. When it became a convict settlement in 1788, New South Wales named a much larger area than the present New South Wales. At that time, for example, it included parts of New Zealand.

Matthew Flinders, the first recorded person to sail around Australia, used the name Terra Australis. However, he said he preferred the name Australia which he knew some people were using. In 1804, Flinders decided to put Australia on his famous map of the coastline. The name gradually became more popular and in 1824 the name Australia was officially approved by the British Admiralty.

1 Roman times took place

- **A** not long ago.
- **B** a long time ago.
- **C** very recently.
- **D** a year or two back.

2 Why was the name 'Unknown Land to the South' used in the past?

- **A** It sounded important.
- **B** It was well known.
- **C** People were uncertain if the south land existed.
- **D** It was a friendly sounding name.

3 Why did the Dutch use the name New Holland for parts of Australia?

- **A** They got tired of using a Latin name.
- **B** They didn't like the name New South Wales.
- **C** The Dutch planned to shift Holland to this new place.
- **D** They named it for their own country, Holland.

4 How was New South Wales in the late 1700s different from New South Wales today?

- **A** It was home to Dutch explorers.
- **B** It named a much larger area of land at that time.
- **C** There were no differences.
- **D** It covered a smaller areas in the late 1700s.

5 What does the name Australia, taken from the Latin word *Australis*, mean?

....

6 Why didn't Matthew Flinders use the name New Holland or New South Wales for the country he sailed all the way around?

....

....

....

Answers and explanations on pp. 101–102

Step-by-step guide to **language** questions

Language questions involve examining how language is used in a text.

Use this **Step-by-step guide** to help you read the text and examine the way **language** is used to answer the questions below. Circle the correct answers or write your answer on the lines.

STEP 1	**Skim** the text to see what it is about and how it is organised.	**Read** the title, '*Ships of the desert*'. Notice that there are inverted commas around the title. Look at the illustration and think about how it relates to the title. Look at other visual elements. Notice that the text is in paragraphs. Make **predictions** about the subject and purpose of the text.
STEP 2	**Read** the text. **Monitor** your reading to make sure you understand the text.	**Visualise** and **connect** with the ideas in the text**. Think** about what you already know about the subject and the type of text, a report. Make **predictions.** Make **inferences**. Reflect on meanings and make **judgements**.

'Ships of the desert'

In outback Australia, in the mid-19th century, bullocks, horses and donkeys were the main means of transport. The problem was that these animals were not well suited to journeys over long distances, particularly in harsh, dry, desert conditions.

It was well known that camels could carry heavy loads and survive for days at a time without food or water. Could these 'ships of the desert' be used to help solve Australia's transport problems?

Early experiments with imported camels were successful and soon most Australian states were importing single-humped dromedaries from places such as India and Afghanistan. Afghan cameleers, Muslim men who were skilled at managing camels, were also brought into Australia.

Soon camel teams were journeying with explorers, moving wool from sheep stations to railways, hauling wagons with supplies and equipment and carting mail and supplies to remote areas. They were employed to help with major construction projects such as the Overland Telegraph and the Trans-Australian Railway, known as The Ghan.

By the mid-1900s, when railway systems and motorised transport were better developed, camels were no longer needed. Many camels were released into the wild. Now there was a new problem for Australia—an ever-multiplying population of feral camels.

Question 1 **What is the answer to the question asked by the text?**

A Yes, because camels weren't strong.
B Yes, because camels were very hardy and tough.
C No, because camels couldn't survive in the desert.
D No, because camels are feral.

STEP		
STEP ③	**Read** the question. **Think** about what type of question it is. Work out what you need to do to answer it.	This is a **language** question. You need to find the question asked in the text. Then you need to decide which of the suggested options is correct.
STEP ④	**Think** about the text. Remember what you have read and **visualised**.	**Scan** the text to find the question that is asked. Re-read the text and **think** about the answer.

B is correct. This is a **language** question. The question asked is *Could these 'ships of the desert' be used to help solve Australia's transport problems?* (see lines 10–12). The answer in the text is that yes, the camels could help solve the problems because they are so tough and hardy.

Check the other options to confirm they are incorrect. **A** is incorrect because the camels were strong. **C** and **D** are incorrect because the answer is yes rather than no and the reasons given are wrong.

Question 2 Camels are described as 'ships of the desert' because

A they look like cargo ships.
B they transport people and goods through the desert.
C they sail across the desert.
D their humps are shaped like waves.

STEP		
STEP ③	**Read** the question. **Think** about what type of question it is. Work out what you need to do to answer it.	This is a **language** question. You need to work out the reason for camels being called 'ships of the desert'. Look for information in the text that explains this. Look at the illustration for clues.
STEP ④	**Think** about the text. Remember what you have read and **visualised**.	Look at how the words 'ships of the desert' are used. Think about why there are inverted commas around the words in the text. Think about whether camels are compared to ships because of their appearance or because of what they do.

B is correct. This is a **language** question. The inverted commas show that camels are not really 'ships of the desert', but are like them in some way. The reason is that camels transport people and goods across the desert just as ships transport people and goods across the sea.

Check the other options to confirm they are incorrect. **A** is incorrect because, while camels may look like cargo ships when they are loaded, it is their carrying those loads across the desert that makes them like a ship carrying loads across the sea. **C** is incorrect because the way camels move across the desert is quite unlike the way ships sail. **D** is incorrect because there is no connection between the shape of their humps and the reason they are called 'ships of the desert'.

Question 3 Which of these words does not name a country?

A Australia
B Afghanistan
C India
D Ghan

STEP		
STEP ③	**Read** the question. **Think** about what type of question it is. Work out what you need to do to answer it.	This is a **language** question. You need to work out which of these words is not the name of a country.
STEP ④	**Think** about the text. Remember what you have read and **visualised**.	**Scan** the text for each of the words. Re-read the text that surrounds the words to check whether or not a country is named.

D is correct. This is a **language** question. You read *the Trans-Australian Railway, known as The Ghan* (see line 19). This makes it clear that The Ghan, which is shortened from the word *Afghan*, is the name of a railway and not of a country.

Check the other options to confirm they are incorrect. **A**, **B** and **C** are incorrect as Australia, Afghanistan and India name countries.

Step-by-step guide to **language** questions *continued*

Language questions involve examining how language is used in a text.

'Ships of the desert'

In outback Australia, in the mid-19th century, bullocks, horses and donkeys were the main means of transport. The problem was that these animals were not well suited to journeys over long distances, particularly in harsh, dry, desert conditions.

It was well known that camels could carry heavy loads and survive for days at a time without food or water. Could these 'ships of the desert' be used to help solve Australia's transport problems?

Early experiments with imported camels were successful and soon most Australian states were importing single-humped dromedaries from places such as India and Afghanistan. Afghan cameleers, Muslim men who were skilled at managing camels, were also brought into Australia.

Soon camel teams were journeying with explorers, moving wool from sheep stations to railways, hauling wagons with supplies and equipment and carting mail and supplies to remote areas. They were employed to help with major construction projects such as the Overland Telegraph and the Trans-Australian Railway, known as The Ghan.

By the mid-1900s, when railway systems and motorised transport were better developed, camels were no longer needed. Many camels were released into the wild. Now there was a new problem for Australia—an ever-multiplying population of feral camels.

Question 4

Early experiments with imported camels were successful … ***(line 13)***
The word *imported* means

A brought from one country into another.
B double humped.
C single humped.
D sent out of the country.

STEP 3 **Read** the question. **Think** about what type of question it is. Work out what you need to do to answer it.

- This is a **language** question. You need to examine the context in which the word *imported* is used to work out its meaning.

STEP 4 **Think** about the text. Remember what you have read and **visualised**.

- **Scan** the text to find the word *imported* or any related words. Re-read the paragraph that uses this term to work out whether it means 'brought from one country into another', 'double humped', 'single humped' or 'sent out of the country'.

A is correct. This is a **language** question. You may know that the prefix *im-* often means 'into'. You read *Afghan cameleers … were also brought into Australia* (see lines 14–15). This confirms that *imported* means 'brought from one country into another'.

Check the other options to confirm they are incorrect. **B** and **C** are incorrect because the word *imported* refers here to all camels, not just double- or single-humped camels alone. **D** is incorrect because the camels were brought into Australia rather than sent out of it. You may know that to send goods out of the country (the prefix *ex-* means 'out of') is to export them, whereas to bring them in is to import them.

Question 5 What are feral camels?

A camels who run wild and are untamed
B dromedaries
C pack camels
D 'ships of the desert'

STEP 3 **Read** the question. **Think** about what type of question it is. Work out what you need to do to answer it.

This is a **language** question. You need to work out what feral camels are.

STEP 4 **Think** about the text. Remember what you have read and **visualised**.

Scan the text to find the part that uses the words *feral camels*. Re-read it to work out whether feral camels are camels who run wild and are untamed, dromedaries, pack camels or 'ships of the desert'.

A is correct. This is a **language** question. You read *Many camels were released into the wild* (see line 21). This means that as the camels had babies (multiplied) in the wild, they would grow up running untamed by humans.

Check the other options to confirm they are incorrect. **B** is incorrect as dromedaries are one-humped camels. **C** is incorrect because feral camels would not carry packs in the wild. **D** is incorrect because feral camels do not transport goods across desert areas.

Question 6 What is a *cameleer* (line 15)?

Explain your answer on the lines below.

STEP 3 **Read** the question. **Think** about what type of question it is. Work out what you need to do to answer it.

This is a **language** question. You are being asked to work out what a cameleer is from how the word is used and your understanding of how words are formed.

STEP 4 **Think** about the text. Remember what you have read and **visualised**.

Scan the text to find where the word cameleer is used. Re-read the paragraph and **think** about the information the context gives you. **Think** about the word ending *eer* and how that might change the meaning of *camel*.

The text states that cameleers were brought to Australia because of their skills in managing camels. This suggests a cameleer is a person who manages camels. You may know that the suffix *er* (or in this case *eer*) is often added to a word to describe a job or profession. For example, *puppet—puppeteer*, *engine—engineer*. This would help you work out that a *cameleer* (*camel* + *eer*) is someone who works with camels.

Language questions

Use the **Step-by-step guide** on pages 52–55 to help you read the text and examine the way **language** is used to answer the questions below. Circle the correct answers or write your answer on the lines.

My new puppy

Dear Diary

My new puppy is a Tibetan Terrier. Her name is Tezza and she will arrive here tomorrow. Here is how I plan to take care of her.

1. Keep her in a small space at first. She will be excited but she'll probably be a bit scared until she gets to know us properly.
2. Introduce her to my cat, Whiskers, very carefully. I won't leave them alone together until they are used to each other. (You'll be OK, Whiskers.)
3. Persuade her to sleep in a special bed in the laundry. I've used my old flannelette pjs to line her bed as they're soft and warm. I have a ticking clock ready in case she cries at night. TICK TOCK sounds like her mother's heartbeat, you see.
4. Give her three or four small meals. Do NOT feed Tezza chocolate, onions or raisins as they are poisonous to dogs.
5. Give her clean, fresh water. (I promise I'll wash her bowl every day, Mum.)
6. Play games with her and see she gets lots of exercise. (Tezza, Tezza—I can't wait.)

You can meet her tomorrow, dear Diary. I promise I won't let her eat you :)

Harry

1 A Tibetan Terrier is

A Harry's name for his dog.
B a type of dog.
C a dog who was born in Tibet.
D a toy dog.

2 The verbs used at each step of Harry's plan are

A instructions to himself.
B in the past tense.
C asking questions.
D requests to Tezza.

3 *TICK TOCK sounds like her mother's heartbeat, you see.* (line 16)

When Harry says *you see* he is talking to

A Tezza.
B his Mum.
C his diary.
D Whiskers.

4 *(Tezza, Tezza—I can't wait.)* (line 20)

Harry repeats Tezza's name because

A he is practising his pronunciation of it.
B her second name is Tezza.
C he is proud of her name.
D he is so excited at the thought of her arrival.

5 *I promise I won't let her eat you :)* (line 21)

Why does Harry add a smiley face to his comment?

....

....

....

....

Answers and explanations on pp. 102–103

Language questions

Use the **Step-by-step guide** on pages 52–55 to help you read the text and examine the way **language** is used to answer the questions below. Circle the correct answers or write your answer on the lines.

In the olden days

Molly: Gran, did you get chicken pox when you were little?

Gran: I certainly did, Molly. I was home from school for ten days.

Molly: I'm so glad I've been vaccinated. I've heard you get really itchy and you're not allowed to scratch.

Gran: Can you see this minute white patch on my cheek? That's a chicken-pox scar.

Molly: *You* scratched!

Gran: Yes, I'm afraid so. I also had baths with crystals that made the water pink.

Molly: What did you do all day? Did you watch TV?

Gran: We didn't have TV then.

Molly: What! I knew you didn't have the internet or mobiles in the olden days. But no TV. That must have been terrible.

Gran: Not at all. What you don't have, you don't miss. We did have a radio and I listened to *The Argonauts*. I read books and comics. I played Fiddlesticks and Jacks and card games. I even had a midnight feast one night with my sisters. Don't tell your mother that last bit. She'll say I'm a 'Bad Influence'!

Molly: I won't, Gran. That's a good idea though. Can we play Snakes and Ladders now?

Gran: Yes. And then I'll teach you Clock Patience. It's a game my Gran taught me. It's one you can play all by yourself.

1 *I certainly did, Molly.* (line 3)

The modal word *certainly* makes Gran's answer

- **A** very definite.
- **B** highly unlikely.
- **C** a bit doubtful.
- **D** fairly sure.

2 *Can you see this minute white patch on my cheek?* (line 7)

The word *minute* means

- **A** easily seen.
- **B** large.
- **C** extremely small.
- **D** middling sized.

3 *You scratched!* (line 9)

Molly's exclamation shows

- **A** anger.
- **B** fear.
- **C** sorrow.
- **D** surprise.

4 *What you don't have, you don't miss.* (line 17)

This sentence is

- **A** an exclamation.
- **B** an old saying.
- **C** a simile.
- **D** a metaphor.

5 *The Argonauts* (line 18) was

- **A** a next-door family.
- **B** a programme on TV.
- **C** a radio programme.
- **D** a noisy game.

6 Why do the words '*Bad Influence*' (line 20) have capital letters?

....

....

....

Answers and explanations on p. 103

Language questions

Use the **Step-by-step guide** on pages 52–55 to help you read the text and examine the way **language** is used to answer the questions below. Circle the correct answers or write your answer on the lines.

Country life versus city life

My name is Bertie. I want to argue that country life is much better than city life.

To begin with, who would choose pongy pollution and petrol fumes over fresh air that smells of cut hay and eucalyptus? Certainly not me.

Then there's the noise. Cities are full of noisy cars and trucks and screeching sirens. The country is usually peaceful and quiet—the gentle mooing of cows, some magpies singing perhaps. Heavenly!

And what about all the space you have when living in the country? Your cranky neighbours aren't next door listening and watching your every move. Your pets are not shut up all day inside while you go to school.

In the country there's space to ride your horse or your bike, run in the fields, fish in the streams, walk in the hills. I love being outside with my sheepdog, Bruno, and my horse, Spirit. We have the best times together.

Country people are famous for their community feeling. They aren't always in a rush like city people. They have time to help out others, time for family, time to do things together. Country life is better. No question.

1 *... who would choose pongy pollution and petrol fumes over fresh air ...?* (line 3)

This question is worded to encourage the reply that

- **A** everybody would.
- **B** nobody would.
- **C** anybody would.
- **D** all would.

2 *Certainly not me.* (line 4)

The modal word *Certainly* makes Bertie's statement sound

- **A** more definite.
- **B** less definite.
- **C** no different.
- **D** not very likely.

3 Which words suggest Bertie could be exaggerating? Choose all that apply.

- **A** cranky
- **B** mooing of cows
- **C** screeching
- **D** space to ride

4 *to ride ... run ... fish ... walk* (line 17)

These verbs describe .... that Bertie enjoys in the country.

- **A** memories
- **B** moods
- **C** thoughts
- **D** actions

5 Bertie concludes his speech with *No question*. What does he mean?

....

....

....

....

Answers and explanations on p. 103

Language questions

Use the **Step-by-step guide** on pages 52–55 to help you read the text and examine the way **language** is used to answer the questions below. Circle the correct answers or write your answer on the lines.

City life versus country life

My name is Lian. I'm a city girl. I can't imagine living miles from everything I like to see and do.

Bertie praised the country air but there's plenty of fresh air in the city. We have parks and bushland and special reserves all over the place. There can be a little bit of pollution but it's never too bad. Also you can easily get to places that are always fun and interesting.

Bertie likes the quiet of the country. It's nice sometimes. But I also like the sounds of things moving about—ferries honking their horns, buskers singing, the ice-cream van playing 'Greensleeves'.

We like having neighbours right next door. They don't get in our hair. And we are close to everything—movies, museums, shops, skateboard ramps, beaches. The list is endless.

I also like playing on my computer and using my mobile phone. The connections aren't always good in the country and you can feel really isolated when you can't get online to connect with people.

I'm sure you'll agree with me—city life is magical.

1. *There can be a little bit of pollution …* (line 4)

   Lian describes pollution this way because she wants to

   A show how bad it is.
   B make it sound worse than it is.
   C minimise how bad it can be.
   D describe it accurately.

2. *It's nice sometimes.* (line 6)

   This comment shows Lian thinks that Bertie

   A always tells lies.
   B exaggerates the whole time.
   C has said something she can partly accept.
   D always tells the truth.

3. *the ice-cream van playing 'Greensleeves'* (line 7)

   'Greensleeves' names a

   A person. **B** place.
   C song. **D** game.

4. *[The neighbours] don't get in our hair.* (line 8)

   This means Lian thinks her neighbours are

   A useless. **B** never a problem.
   C annoying. **D** pests.

5. What does *isolated* (line 11) mean?

   ....

   ....

Answers and explanations on p. 104

Language questions

Use the **Step-by-step guide** on pages 52–55 to help you read the text and examine the way **language** is used to answer the questions below. Circle the correct answers or write your answer on the lines.

The whistling language

Hotel Tenerife
Tenerife
Canary Islands

Hi Timmy

Last weekend Uncle Graham and I visited La Gomera, one of the smallest of the Canary Islands. I wanted to tell you about their whistling language.

Because La Gomera is so mountainous, its people have always communicated with each other across the gorges by whistling. The different races who have lived there use it to report news or tell about coming events such as weddings or baptisms. The whistlers use their fingers to change the shape of their mouths to make the sounds of the syllables.

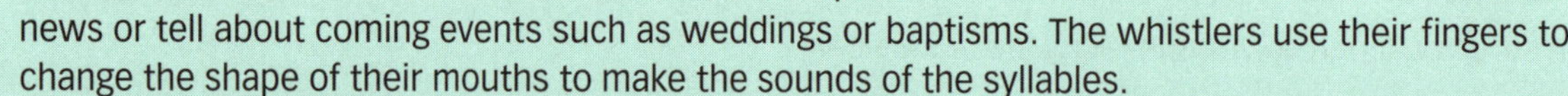

I talked to a young Spanish boy called Cyro about el silbo (the whistle). He told me that the whistling language used to be known by everyone. When it began to die out some time ago, the local government made it compulsory for children to spend four years in primary school learning to whistle in Gomeran.

I found a UNESCO video on YouTube that shows a classroom of children practising Gomeran whistling. Perhaps you might like to watch it.

We'll be back Down Under, in dear old Oz, very soon.

Love to all

Auntie Chris

PS The Canary Islands got its name from dogs (*canaris* in Latin) on the islands, not canaries!

1 Gomeran Whistling is a language used

A in everyday conversations.
B at baptisms.
C to communicate over long distances.
D only as a hobby.

2 Which of the following is Spanish?

A YouTube
B el silbo
C canaris
D UNESCO

3 *We'll be back Down Under … very soon.* *(line 20)*

Where is Down Under?

A back in bed under the clothes
B back in Australia
C back down off the mountains
D back in the valley

4 *Perhaps you might like to watch it.* *(line 19)*

These words are given

A as an order.
B in a forceful way.
C very insistently.
D as a suggestion.

5 What feelings do Auntie Chris's words show she holds towards Australia?

....

....

....

....

....

Answers and explanations on p. 104

Language questions

Use the **Step-by-step guide** on pages 52–55 to help you read the text and examine the way **language** is used to answer the questions below. Circle the correct answers or write your answer on the lines.

Jake's jokes

The Editor
CHATTER

Dear Editor

In last month's *CHATTER* you asked your readers to send in their favourite jokes. I'm sending you a list of my favourites. I hope you like them.

Jake Swinnerton

1. Q: What do you do with a blue elephant?
A: You try and cheer it up.

2. **Q:** What do you name a camel with no humps?
A: Humphrey.

3. **Q:** Why didn't the skeleton go to the disco?
A: Because he had nobody to go with.

4. **Q:** Why do birds fly south in the winter?
A: Sorry, I forget the answer. But I know it makes me laugh.

5. **Q:** Did you hear about the magic tractor?
A: It went down the lane and turned into a field.

6. Q: What does a snail say when it's riding on a turtle's back?
A: Wheeeee!!

1. In Joke number 1 *blue* means both the colour and
   - **A** large.
   - **B** happy.
   - **C** sad.
   - **D** peculiar.
2. Joke number 2 is mainly funny because Humphrey
   - **A** is not a camel's name.
   - **B** sounds similar to hump free.
   - **C** is hard to spell.
   - **D** is difficult to pronounce.
3. Which words create the humour in the answer to Joke number 3?
   - **A** Because
   - **B** he had
   - **C** nobody
   - **D** to go with
4. The answer Jake forgets in Joke number 4 is
   - **A** Their instinct takes them there.
   - **B** They go there for food and shelter.
   - **C** They are moving to a warmer climate.
   - **D** Because it's too far to walk.
5. Which words create the humour of the answer to Joke number 5?
   - **A** It went
   - **B** down the lane and
   - **C** turned into
   - **D** a field.
6. Why is Joke number 6 funny?

   ....

   ....

   ....

Answers and explanations on pp. 104–105

Language questions

Use the **Step-by-step guide** on pages 52–55 to help you read the text and examine the way **language** is used to answer the questions below. Circle the correct answers or write your answer on the lines.

Hangout@Holly's

www.hangout@holly's.com.qld.au

Hangout@Holly's

- Affordable prices
- A retro rural restaurant mainly for tweens and teens
- Comfy Cool Chic

Menu

Try the fresh food bar: avos, baby spinach, potato salad, hard-boiled eggs (laid today!), newly baked bread, butter from our own cows. Choose a picnic and have it in our garden.

Try the juicy juice bar: Dreamy combinations such as rhubarb and apple, mango and passion fruit. It's your choice when you Hangout@Holly's.

Try the delectable desserts: strawberries, raspberries, pears, peaches, apricots (just picked and bursting with goodness and sunshine). Dress your choice with clotted cream or homemade ice-cream.

Read more ...

Special Events

Have a Hangout@Holly's party for your next birthday

Bring your mum to a Mother's Day breakfast

Halloween coming? Book into Hangout@Holly's for supper by lantern light (in pumpkins, of course ...)

Read more ...

Just drop by or make a reservation

Phone: (07) 9944 0304 • Address: 234 The Backway, Montvillier, Queensland

Click here for a map

1 The name Hangout@Holly's suggests that the atmosphere of this restaurant will be

A formal. **B** casual.
C romantic. **D** traditional.

2 What is emphasised about the restaurant in this text? Choose all that apply.

A the freshness of the food
B the ease of getting there
C the healthy choices available
D how inexpensive it is

3 Which of these provides a factual description? Choose all that apply.

A fruit—bursting with goodness and sunshine
B bread—newly baked
C ice-cream—homemade
D juices—dreamy combinations

4 *hard-boiled eggs (laid today!)* (line 10)

What does this statement tell you?

A The chickens laid hard-boiled eggs.
B The restaurant only serves eggs laid that day.
C The restaurant boils the eggs daily.
D The chickens laid fresh eggs.

5 What shows that this is a website rather than a print advertisement?

....

....

Answers and explanations on pp. 105–106

Language questions

Use the **Step-by-step guide** on pages 52–55 to help you read the text and examine the way **language** is used to answer the questions below. Circle the correct answers or write your answer on the lines.

Dot and the Kangaroo

Source: Wikimedia Commons

'I was thinking,' said Dot.

'Oh! don't think!' pleaded the Kangaroo; 'I never do myself.'

'I can't help it!' explained the little girl. 'What do you do instead?' she asked.

'I always jump to conclusions,' said the Kangaroo, and she promptly bounded ten feet at one hop. Lightly springing back again to her position in front of the child, she added, 'And that's why I never have a headache.'

'Dear Kangaroo,' said Dot, 'Do you know where I can get some water? I'm very thirsty!'

'Of course you are,' said her friend; 'Everyone is at sundown. I'm thirsty myself. But the nearest water-hole is a longish way off, so we had better start at once.'

Little Dot got up with an effort. After her long run and fatigue, she was very stiff, and her little legs were so tired and weak, that after a few steps she staggered and fell.

The Kangaroo looked at the child compassionately. 'Poor little Human,' she said … 'Just step into my pouch, and I'll hop you down to the water-hole in less time than it takes a locust to shrill.'

Timidly and carefully, Dot did the Kangaroo's bidding, and found herself in the cosiest, softest little bag imaginable.

From *Dot and the Kangaroo* by Ethel Pedley, 1899

1. Why does the author give the word *Kangaroo* a capital letter?
   - **A** The author thinks that *kangaroo* is spelt with a capital letter.
   - **B** The Kangaroo is not just any kangaroo; she is a character in the story.
   - **C** The story is about a large kangaroo so it has a capital letter.
   - **D** She is the most important kangaroo in her mob.

2. '*I always jump to conclusions*' (line 6)

   What is comical about this saying?
   - **A** The Kangaroo means that she literally jumps to conclusions.
   - **B** It is a simile.
   - **C** It is always comical to hear animals talking.
   - **D** The Kangaroo is behaving like a clown.

3. Which sentence suggests that the Kangaroo thinks Dot is like her?
   - **A** Little Dot got up with an effort.
   - **B** 'What do you do instead?' she asked.
   - **C** 'Everyone is at sundown.'
   - **D** 'I can't help it!' explained the little girl.

4. *The Kangaroo looked at the child compassionately.* (line 15)

   What does *compassionately* mean?
   - **A** unkindly
   - **B** sympathetically
   - **C** keenly
   - **D** enthusiastically

5. *Dot did the Kangaroo's bidding …* (line 17)

   What does this mean?
   - **A** Dot turned away from the Kangaroo.
   - **B** Dot asked the Kangaroo for help.
   - **C** Dot ignored the Kangaroo's advice.
   - **D** Dot did what the Kangaroo had told her to do.

6. Why does the Kangaroo compare the time it will take to get to the water-hole with the time it takes a locust to shrill?

   ....

   ....

Answers and explanations on p. 106

Step-by-step guide to **judgement** questions

Judgement questions involve making judgements.

Use this **Step-by-step guide** to help you read the text and make **judgements** to answer the questions below. Circle the correct answers or write your answer on the lines.

STEP 1 **Skim** the text to see what it is about and how it is organised.	**Read** the title, *Pinocchio*. Notice the date when the story was written and that this is part of a longer story. Look at the illustration and other visual elements. You can **predict** that they are characters in the text. Notice that the text is mainly made up of conversation between two characters. Make **predictions** about the subject and purpose of the text.
STEP 2 **Read** the text. Make sure you understand it.	**Visualise** and **connect** with the ideas in the text**. Think** about what you already know about the subject and the type of text, a narrative. Make **predictions**. Make **inferences**. Reflect on meanings and make **judgements**.

Pinocchio

'And the four pieces—where have you put them?' asked the Fairy.

'I have lost them!' said Pinocchio, but he was telling a lie, for he had them in his pocket.

He had scarcely told the lie when his nose, which was already long, grew at once two inches longer.

'And where did you lose them?'

'In the wood near here.'

At this second lie his nose went on growing.

'If you have lost them in the wood near here,' said the Fairy, 'we will look for them and we shall find them: because everything that is lost in that wood is always found.'

'Ah! Now I remember all about it,' replied the puppet, getting quite confused;

'I didn't lose the four gold pieces, I swallowed them whilst I was drinking your medicine.'

At this lie his nose grew to such an extraordinary length that poor Pinocchio could not move in any direction ...

The Fairy allowed the puppet to cry for a good half-hour over his nose, which could no longer pass through the door of the room. This she did to give him a severe lesson, and to correct him of the disgraceful fault of telling lies—the most disgraceful fault that a boy can have.

Extract from *Pinocchio* by Carlo Collodi, 1883

Question 1 **Who tells the story?**

A Pinocchio B a narrator C the Fairy D a puppet

STEP 3 **Read** the question. **Think** about what type of question it is. Work out what you need to do to answer it.	This is a **judgement** question. You need to make a **judgement** about whose voice it is that you hear telling the story.

STEP 4 **Think** about the text. Remember what you have read and **visualised**.

Look for evidence in the text that tells who is telling the story—whether it is the voice of Pinocchio, a narrator, the Fairy or a puppet. Consider the evidence to make a **judgement**.

B is correct. The Fairy and Pinnochio are characters in the story that is being told by a narrator.

Check the other options to confirm why they are incorrect. **A** is incorrect because Pinocchio does not tell the story. What he says is in speech marks. **C** is incorrect because the Fairy does not tell the story. What she says is in quotation marks. **D** is incorrect because the puppet, Pinocchio, is a character in the story, not the person who tells it.

Question 2 What is the moral of this story?

A Don't put your nose where it isn't wanted.
B Take good care of your money.
C You should always tell the truth.
D Don't cry over spilt milk.

STEP 3 **Read** the question. **Think** about what type of question it is. Work out what you need to do to answer it.

This is a **judgement** question. The lesson is the moral of the story. You need to work out what lesson the story teaches.

STEP 4 **Think** about the text. Remember what you have read and **visualised**.

Re-read the story to work out what lesson it teaches about the right or wrong way to behave. **Think** about how the characters behave and what happens as a result.

C is correct. You judge that the lesson in the story is that people should always tell the truth because to tell lies is to behave in a disgraceful way and leads to unhappiness.

Check the other options to confirm why they are incorrect. **A** is incorrect as the story is not about interfering in other people's affairs. **B** is incorrect. Pinocchio takes good care of his money, but this is not the moral of the story. **D** is incorrect. Pinocchio cries about what has happened to him, but this is not a moral.

Question 3 Which description is NOT true of Pinocchio?

A He tells lies.
B His nose grows when he tells lies.
C He pretends to cry when his nose gets very long.
D He has the four gold pieces in his pocket.

STEP 3 **Read** the question. **Think** about what type of question it is. Work out what you need to do to answer it.

This is a **judgement** question. You need to **judge** whether the descriptions of Pinocchio and his actions are accurate or not.

STEP 4 **Think** about the text. Remember what you have read and **visualised**.

Re-read the whole text. Look for evidence that tells you if Pinocchio tells lies, if his nose grows when he tells lies, if he pretends to cry about his nose growing and if he has four gold pieces in his pocket. Consider the evidence to make a **judgement**.

C is correct. You judge that Pinocchio is not pretending when he cries about his nose. You think he would be very uncomfortable with such a long nose and that he cries for a good half hour shows he is really upset.

Check the other options to confirm why they are incorrect. **A**, **B** and **D** are all true of Pinocchio. **A** is incorrect because Pinocchio does lie. **B** is incorrect because his nose grows when he lies. **D** is incorrect because he does have the gold in his pocket.

Step-by-step guide to **judgement** questions *continued*

Judgement questions involve making judgements.

Pinocchio

'And the four pieces—where have you put them?' asked the Fairy.

'I have lost them!' said Pinocchio, but he was telling a lie, for he had them in his pocket.

He had scarcely told the lie when his nose, which was already long, grew at once two inches longer.

'And where did you lose them?'

'In the wood near here.'

At this second lie his nose went on growing.

'If you have lost them in the wood near here,' said the Fairy, 'we will look for them and we shall find them: because everything that is lost in that wood is always found.'

'Ah! Now I remember all about it,' replied the puppet, getting quite confused;

'I didn't lose the four gold pieces, I swallowed them whilst I was drinking your medicine.'

At this lie his nose grew to such an extraordinary length that poor Pinocchio could not move in any direction …

The Fairy allowed the puppet to cry for a good half-hour over his nose, which could no longer pass through the door of the room. This she did to give him a severe lesson, and to correct him of the disgraceful fault of telling lies—the most disgraceful fault that a boy can have.

Extract from *Pinocchio* by Carlo Collodi, 1883

Question 4 **Pinocchio tells lies about the gold pieces because**

A he really can't remember what he did with them.
B he likes to watch his nose grow longer.
C he wants to keep the gold pieces for himself.
D he likes tricking the Fairy.

STEP 3 **Read** the question. **Think** about what type of question it is. Work out what you need to do to answer it.

This is a **judgement** question. You need to make a **judgement** about the reason Pinocchio tells lies about the gold pieces.

STEP 4 **Think** about the text. Remember what you have read and **visualised**.

Re-read the text and look for clues as to why Pinocchio would lie about the gold pieces. **Think** about which of the reasons suggested gives the best explanation.

C is correct. You judge that since the gold pieces are in Pinocchio's pocket all the time and he keeps telling lies about where they are, he must want to keep them for himself.

Check the other options to confirm why they are incorrect. **A** is incorrect because he knows they are in his pocket. **B** is incorrect because he gets upset about his nose growing longer. **D** is incorrect because there is no evidence he enjoys deceiving the Fairy even though he keeps doing it. He shows confusion rather than pleasure.

Question 5 How does the Fairy behave?

A cruelly B calmly C unfairly D wickedly

STEP 3 **Read** the question. **Think** about what type of question it is. Work out what you need to do to answer it.	This is a **judgement** question. Use evidence from the text to make a judgement about the Fairy's behaviour.
STEP 4 **Think** about the text. Remember what you have read and **visualised**.	Re-read the whole text. **Think** about what kind of person the Fairy is and how and why she behaves towards Pinocchio as she does.

B is correct. You judge that the Fairy stays calm throughout Pinocchio's lies and confusion. She punishes him in a thoughtful way, hoping to help him learn to stop telling lies.

Check the other options to confirm why they are incorrect. **A**, **C** and **D** are incorrect as there is no evidence that the Fairy behaves in a cruel, unfair or wicked way.

Question 6 How likely is it that Pinocchio will be cured of telling lies by the Fairy?

Explain your answer on the lines below.

STEP 3 **Read** the question. **Think** about what type of question it is. Work out what you need to do to answer it.	This is a **judgement** question. You need to make a **judgement** about whether there is any evidence that Pinocchio is likely to be cured of telling lies.
STEP 4 **Think** about the text. Remember what you have read and **visualised**.	Re-read the text to look for evidence of the Fairy's gifts and whether Pinocchio learns from his mistakes. **Think** about what you know of Pinocchio's habits and character.

Pinocchio does seem very sorry for his actions so it is just possible that the Fairy's punishment might cure him. However, it seems more likely that he won't be cured because telling lies comes so naturally to him. (If you know the story of Pinocchio, you will know it is almost impossible to cure him of lying.)

Judgement questions

Use the **Step-by-step guide** on pages 64–67 to help you read the text and make **judgements** to answer the questions below. Circle the correct answers or write your answer on the lines.

Matilda

Matilda told such Dreadful Lies,
It made one Gasp and Stretch one's Eyes;
Her Aunt, who, from her Earliest Youth,
Had kept a Strict Regard for Truth,
Attempted to Believe Matilda:
The effort very nearly killed her,
And would have done so, had not She
Discovered this Infirmity.
For once, towards the Close of Day,
Matilda, growing tired of play,
And finding she was left alone,
Went tiptoe to the Telephone
And summoned the Immediate Aid
Of London's Noble Fire-Brigade.

…

They galloped, roaring through the Town,
'Matilda's House is Burning Down!'
Inspired by British Cheers and Loud
Proceeding from the Frenzied Crowd,
They ran their ladders through a score
Of windows on the Ball Room Floor;
And took Peculiar Pains to Souse
The Pictures up and down the House,
Until Matilda's Aunt succeeded
In showing them they were not needed
And even then she had to pay
To get the Men to go away!

…

That night a Fire did break out —
You should have heard Matilda Shout!
You should have heard her Scream and Bawl,
And throw the window up and call
To People passing in the Street —
(The rapidly increasing Heat
Encouraging her to obtain
Their confidence)—but all in vain!
For every time She shouted 'Fire!'
They only answered 'Little Liar!'
And therefore when her Aunt returned,
Matilda, and the House, were Burned.

From 'Matilda' by Hilaire Belloc, 1907

1. The action takes place in London in
   - **A** a hovel.
   - **B** a mansion.
   - **C** a farmhouse.
   - **D** a small terrace house.

2. Matilda's actions are
   - **A** dangerous.
   - **B** playful.
   - **C** amusing.
   - **D** thoughtful.

3. The use of rhyme in this cautionary tale emphasises its
   - **A** seriousness.
   - **B** tragedy.
   - **C** bitterness.
   - **D** humour.

4. Matilda's Aunt is NOT
   - **A** trusting.
   - **B** well off.
   - **C** a good citizen.
   - **D** bad tempered.

5. What is the moral of this cautionary tale?

   ....

   ....

   ....

   ....

   ....

   ....

Answers and explanations on pp. 106–107

Judgement questions

Use the **Step-by-step guide** on pages 64–67 to help you read the text and make **judgements** to answer the questions below. Circle the correct answers or write your answer on the lines.

Blogging about bags

Belinda's Blog

May 4, 2015 by Belinda | 7 Comments

I used to think the plastic bags my family carried our shopping in were helpful, harmless things, but now I know better. The shocking truth is that each year more than an estimated* one million seabirds and 100 000 marine mammals die from swallowing, or getting entangled in, plastic bags.

I recently saw a sign saying each shopper uses up to 500 plastic bags a year. Then I found out that each year more than 500 billion plastic bags are consumed on our planet.

I also found out that plastic bags do not biodegrade. This means they can't be fully broken down by nature. They stay in the environment for centuries leaching poisons into the soil and water. And plastic bags are made from oil—more waste.

I've explained all of this to my family. Together we've decided to:

- use ONLY cloth or paper bags for shopping
- put reminders everywhere to take these shopping bags with us
- petition the government to ban free single-use plastic bags in shops. China and India have already done this.

Any other ideas? **Read more**

*roughly judged number

1 Belinda's attitude to plastic bags changes because

A she learns to appreciate them.
B she's always changing her mind.
C she learns much more about them.
D she starts a blog to discuss them.

2 The number of animals that die is estimated because

A Belinda couldn't count them all.
B the researchers can't know the exact number.
C Belinda is using a scientific term to show off.
D the researchers have no idea how many animals die.

3 When Belinda refers to the *shocking truth* *(line 4)* she is describing the situation

A accurately. **B** exaggeratedly.
C carelessly. **D** inaccurately.

4 Belinda's family's response to her information about plastic bags is

A unenthusiastic. **B** disapproving.
C bored. **D** supportive.

5 Plastic bags not biodegrading makes the situation

A even more serious. **B** less serious.
C no different. **D** of no concern.

6 How likely is it that Belinda and her family will stick to their plan? Explain the reasons for your answer.

....

....

....

....

Answers and explanations on p. 107

Judgement questions

Use the **Step-by-step guide** on pages 64–67 to help you read the text and make **judgements** to answer the questions below. Circle the correct answers or write your answer on the lines.

Fire at magic shop

21 AUGUST, 2015

Firefighters were called to a fire in a magic shop in the CBD last night. The magic shop was located on the second floor of a building in Trick Street, Conjure Park. Several fire crews were needed to put out the blaze.

There is still mystery surrounding how the fire began. According to neighbours' reports, no-one was in the building at the time.

'I'm very puzzled about this,' Mrs Spell, the owner of the magic shop, commented. 'How can a fire begin if there is no-one there to begin it?'

'I think something funny is going on,' her assistant, Mr Black, added. 'The damage disappeared in a puff of smoke. Yet the fire raged quite fiercely for several hours.'

The chief of the fire brigade, Mr Quench, also confessed the blaze was not like any he'd come across before. 'In the end the fire just disappeared into thin air,' he stated. 'I only wish all the fires we attended were like this.'

Police are continuing their investigations.

1. The names of the people in this news item make the article
   - **A** more believable.
   - **B** more serious.
   - **C** unbelievable.
   - **D** confusing.

2. The address of the magic shop is included
   - **A** to alert the reader that the report is not serious.
   - **B** to help out those looking for the shop.
   - **C** to pinpoint the location of the shop.
   - **D** to provide correct information about the address.

3. The attitude Mrs Spell takes to the fire breaking out is
   - **A** satisfied.
   - **B** amused.
   - **C** bewildered.
   - **D** pleased.

4. The attitude Mr Black takes to the fire breaking out is
   - **A** suspicious.
   - **B** horrified.
   - **C** disappointed.
   - **D** sad.

5. What makes this news article amusing?

....

....

....

....

....

....

Answers and explanations on pp. 107–108

Judgement questions

Use the **Step-by-step guide** on pages 64–67 to help you read the text and make **judgements** to answer the questions below. Circle the correct answers or write your answer on the lines.

The Swagman

Oh, he was old and he was spare;
His bushy whiskers and his hair
Were all fussed up and very grey
He said he'd come a long, long way
And had a long, long way to go.
Each boot was broken at the toe,
And he'd a swag upon his back.
His billy-can, as black as black,
Was just the thing for making tea
At picnics, so it seemed to me.

'Twas hard to earn a bite of bread,
He told me. Then he shook his head,
And all the little corks that hung
Around his hat-brim danced and swung
And bobbed about his face; and when
I laughed he made them dance again.
He said they were for keeping flies —
'The pesky varmints'—from his eyes.
He called me 'Codger'... 'Now you see
The best days of your life,' said he.
'But days will come to bend your back,
And, when they come, keep off the track.
Keep off, young codger, if you can.'
He seemed a funny sort of man.

...

I sometimes think: When I'm a man,
I'll get a good black billy-can
And hang some corks around my hat,
And lead a jolly life like that.

From A *Book for Kids* by CJ Dennis, 1921

1 Who is the narrator of this poem?

A an old man
B a young boy
C an elderly poet
D a swagman

2 What is the boy's attitude to the swagman's billy-can?

A hostile **B** grateful
C admiring **D** resentful

3 How does the swagman feel looking back at his life?

A contented **B** pleased
C proud **D** regretful

4 Why does the swagman make his corks bob a second time?

A The flies were annoying him.
B It was a habit of his.
C He wanted to please the boy and make him laugh again.
D He was shaking his head sadly.

5 What makes the boy think the swagman's life is jolly?

Answers and explanations on p. 108

Judgement questions

Use the **Step-by-step guide** on pages 64–67 to help you read the text and make **judgements** to answer the questions below. Circle the correct answers or write your answer on the lines.

An advertisement from 1900

Source: Wikipedia

1. What is being advertised?
   - **A** pears (the fruit)
   - **B** soap
   - **C** pets
   - **D** children's shoes

2. The advertisers want viewers to think this child is
   - **A** happy and well cared for.
   - **B** sad and grubby.
   - **C** living in poverty.
   - **D** dirty and neglected.

3. The setting links Pears soap with families who
   - **A** allow rough dogs into their good rooms.
   - **B** are well off and respectable.
   - **C** have very naughty children.
   - **D** adopt stray animals.

4. How do you know this is not a modern advertisement? Choose all that apply.
   - **A** The child's clothing is from an earlier time.
   - **B** The dog has a bow around its neck.
   - **C** The washing basin is old fashioned.
   - **D** The room looks comfortable and cosy.

5. Who was the advertisement mainly aimed at?

....

....

....

....

 Answers and explanations on pp. 108–109

Judgement questions

Use the **Step-by-step guide** on pages 64–67 to help you read the text and make **judgements** to answer the questions below. Circle the correct answers or write your answer on the lines.

The perils of palm oil

www.palmoilproductions.com

About us | Contact us | Latest news

Palm oil:

- is a vegetable oil made from the fruit of the palm tree.
- is found in many packaged items on supermarket shelves. Think: chips, biscuits, margarine, toothpaste, shampoo, cooking oil, etc.
- grows in tropical areas in Africa, Asia, North America and South America. Malaysia and Indonesia currently provide around 85% of global palm-oil production.

Trees can be grown in a sustainable way but often the methods used are destructive.

Many labels do not reveal whether or not the products contain palm oil.

90% of orang-utan habitats have been destroyed in the last twenty years.

Did you know?

- According to the World Wildlife Fund, an area of about 300 football fields of rainforest is cleared each hour to make way for palm oil production. By 2020 the demand for palm oil is expected to double.
- The release of gases from deforestation causes pollution and health problems.
- Unless deforestation is prevented, animal numbers will continue to decrease.

What can YOU do? Click **here** to find out.

1. In the future, the demand for palm oil is likely to
   A increase. **B** decrease.
   C stay about the same. **D** disappear.

2. Why is an image of an orang-utan included on the website? Choose all that apply.
   A to catch the viewers' attention
   B to show the viewer what an orang-utan looks like
   C to appeal to the viewer's emotions
   D to show there is a link between palm oil and orang-utans

3. Which item would NOT be suitable to add to the *Latest news* (line 3) link?
   A news about an improved labelling system for palm-oil products
   B new calculations about the percentages of endangered animal species
   C news about a new chain of supermarkets
   D new research about the causes of climate change

4. Information on this website is made more believable by
   A the use of exaggerated language.
   B the backing of a claim by a respected organisation.
   C the use of a lot of information and statistics.
   D the inclusion of the picture of an orang-utan.

5. What suggestions might you find linked to the word *here* (line 32) on this website? Name two or three.

....

....

....

Answers and explanations on p. 109

Judgement questions

Use the **Step-by-step guide** on pages 64–67 to help you read the text and make **judgements** to answer the questions below. Circle the correct answers or write your answer on the lines.

Natural wonders

Famous natural wonders of Australia include:

- **The Great Barrier Reef**, off the coast of Queensland. This is the world's largest coral reef. It is over 25 million years old and stretches for 3000 kilometres. It is home to coral gardens, hundreds of islands and a rich variety of marine life including humpback whales. Environmental threats to the Reef have prompted strong protests about the government's failure to properly protect this natural wonder.
- **Uluru**, in the Northern Territory. This is a sandstone monolith and sacred site for First Nations people. It was formed around 600 million years ago. It stands 348 metres above sea level and is 9.4 kilometres in circumference. It is famous for the beauty of its changing colours. In 1985 ownership was returned to local First Australians. It is now leased by them to National Parks and Wildlife, and managed jointly with the Australian government.
- **The Twelve Apostles**, off the Victorian coast. These are limestone stacks rising from the ocean. Around 10–20 million years ago they were part of cliffs on the mainland. Storms and winds eroded the sandstone, forming large limestone caves. As these collapsed, towering stacks of rock up to 45 metres high were left behind. Today there are only eight 'apostles' still standing.

1 What is natural about these wonders?

A They are unusual.
B They are part of nature.
C They earn money for their owners.
D They are environments that need special care.

2 What is NOT true of all three natural wonders?

A They are located in Australia.
B They are tourist attractions.
C They have a long history.
D They are sacred sites.

3 The attitude of the author to environmental problems is

A concerned.
B highly anxious.
C unconcerned.
D despairing.

4 What has made all three of the natural wonders famous?

A They are man-made attractions.
B They are under serious environmental threat.
C They are at least ten million years old.
D They are owned by the government.

5 Would this text be suitable as an advertisement to attract tourists? Explain the reasons for your answer.

Answers and explanations on pp. 109–110

Judgement questions

Use the **Step-by-step guide** on pages 64–67 to help you read the text and make **judgements** to answer the questions below. Circle the correct answers or write your answer on the lines.

Clancy of the Overflow

I had written him a letter which I had, for
want of better
Knowledge, sent to where I met him down
the Lachlan*, years ago,
He was shearing when I knew him, so I sent
the letter to him,
Just 'on spec', addressed as follows:
'Clancy, of The Overflow'.*
And an answer came directed in a writing
unexpected,
(And I think the same was written in a
thumbnail dipped in tar)
'Twas his shearing mate who wrote it, and
verbatim* I will quote it:
'Clancy's gone to Queensland droving, and
we don't know where he are.'
In my wild erratic fancy visions come to me
of Clancy
Gone a-droving 'down the Cooper'* where the
western drovers go;
As the stock are slowly stringing, Clancy rides
behind them singing,
For the drover's life has pleasures that the
townsfolk never know.
…
And I somehow rather fancy that I'd like to
change with Clancy,
Like to take a turn at droving where the seasons
come and go,
While he faced the round eternal of the
cash-book and the journal —
But I doubt he'd suit the office, Clancy, of
The Overflow.

From 'Clancy of the Overflow' by AB 'Banjo' Paterson, 1889

*The Lachlan is a river in New South Wales.
*The Overflow was a sheep station.
**Verbatim* means 'word for word'.
*The Cooper is a creek in Queensland.

1. The narrator addresses his letter to Clancy of the Overflow because he
   - **A** knew his name was enough to find him.
   - **B** thought the postman wouldn't need a full address.
   - **C** couldn't remember his address.
   - **D** hoped his name was enough to find him.

2. The narrator says the answer was unexpected because
   - **A** it was not written in ink.
   - **B** it was written by Clancy's shearing mate.
   - **C** it arrived after a very long time.
   - **D** it brought good news.

3. The narrator sees Clancy as someone who is
   - **A** a rowdy bushman.
   - **B** a humble character.
   - **C** a bit of a legend.
   - **D** his best friend.

4. What does the narrator know about Clancy's life as a drover?
   - **A** He droves near the Cooper Creek.
   - **B** He sings when he's droving.
   - **C** The narrator knows nothing at all about it.
   - **D** He finds it a pleasurable life.

5. What makes the narrator fancy he'd like to change with Clancy?

   ....

   ....

   ....

   ....

Answers and explanations on p. 110

BRINGING IT ALL TOGETHER

Mixed questions

Use the **Step-by-step guide** on page 4 to help you read the text and then answer the questions below. Circle the correct answers or write your answer on the lines.

Bees

Bees are flying insects. Like all insects, their bodies have three parts—a head, a thorax and an abdomen. They have five eyes, two sets of wings and three pairs of legs. The hair that covers a bee's body, including parts of its eyes, collects pollen. Bees scrape this pollen into pollen 'baskets' attached to the outsides of their back legs.

There are many different species of bees. Those that live in hives, such as the honey bee, make a honeycomb of cells inside the hive where they store nectar and the queen bee's eggs.

The queen bee is the 'head' of the society. She lays thousands of eggs. Drones, male bees, make up about five per cent of the bee community. Their main job is to mate with the queen bee. The workers, female bees, have different functions including making honeycomb cells for storage, feeding the queen bee and her larvae, keeping the hive clean and cool, and collecting nectar and pollen. They work hard and sometimes they literally die from exhaustion.

Scout bees search for the best places to find nectar. For bees to fill their stomachs with nectar, they have to visit about 2000 flowers. When they return to the hive they do a waggling dance that tells other bees where to go to find nectar.

1 Which piece of information is evidence that the bee is an insect?
- **A** It has five eyes.
- **B** It has hair on its body.
- **C** It can sting.
- **D** It has three parts to its body.

2 Bees' eyes are unusual because
- **A** they are used to store pollen.
- **B** they can smell the presence of other bees.
- **C** hairs grow from them.
- **D** they can see in the dark.

3 Which of the following statements is true?
- **A** The queen bee is not very important.
- **B** Drones do all the work.
- **C** Bees enjoy dancing together.
- **D** Each member of a bee hive has its own work to do.

4 Which of the following statements is untrue?
- **A** Not all bees are from the same species.
- **B** Bees fill their stomachs with honey within minutes.
- **C** The honeycomb cells provide safe storage.
- **D** Some bees die from working too hard.

5 Do bees communicate with each other? Explain the reasons for your answer.

....

....

....

....

Answers and explanations on p. 111

Mixed questions

Use the **Step-by-step guide** on page 4 to help you read the text and then answer the questions below. Circle the correct answers or write your answer on the lines.

Fact file: bees

Did you know these facts about the history of bees and how they behave?

- In ancient Egypt the bee was a royal symbol of the pharaoh. In other societies the bee has been thought of as a sacred insect.
- Bee fossils date back over 100 million years. They have been found in many places including ancient Egypt, ancient Greece and Asia. There are also cave paintings of bees, dating back 30 000 years.
- Many species of bees are solitary and don't live in hives.
- Bees are not aggressive but they will sting you if they are threatened. Only female bees have a sting. When a bee stings it dies soon afterwards. The stings can be fatal for people with allergies.
- Without bees, there would be much less food produced. Bees pollinate many of the plants that we eat. Pollination happens when pollen is transferred from the male to the female part of a plant. This allows fertilisation so that seeds can be produced and new plants grow.
- Threats to bees are many and varied. They include drought, pesticides and pollution, loss of habitats and diseases. Recently, whole colonies of bees have suddenly disappeared in some countries. People are puzzled about the explanation and worried about the consequences.

1 This information about bees is organised as a series of

A stories. **B** arguments.
C facts. **D** ideas.

2 Choose all that apply. The consequences of a bee sting include

A the bee dying soon after the sting.
B the bee stinging a second time.
C the possibility of the person getting an infection.
D the possibility of an allergic reaction, and even death.

3 Which statement is untrue of bees?

A Male bees have no sting.
B Pharaohs used the bee as a symbol of royalty.
C All bees live in hives.
D Loss of habitat is a threat to bees.

4 What is the likely result of pollination?

A dead bees
B seeds forming new plants
C plants dying off
D bees getting angry

5 Why are people concerned about whole colonies of bees disappearing?

....

....

....

....

....

Answers and explanations on pp. 111–112

Mixed questions

Use the **Step-by-step guide** on page 4 to help you read the text and then answer the questions below. Circle the correct answers or write your answer on the lines.

Just in Time (Part 1)

Tom badly wanted a kitten. The cat next door had just had kittens. His parents told him to stay away from them.

Every day, Tom crept through a hole in the fence to visit the kittens. Billy, an orange kitten, was the one he liked best. Billy liked to rub his nose against Tom's leg. He had a very loud purr!

One day, Tom hid Billy under his jumper and took him to school. He hid him in his desk. He took off his jumper and squeezed that into the desk as well. There was a round hole in the corner of Tom's desk where an inkwell used to sit. Billy could breathe through that. He was soon asleep.

Mr Brown, Tom's teacher, was chalking some figures on the blackboard. The class was silent for once, working at Maths. Mr Brown noticed a vibratory sound somewhere nearby and turned around.

'What's that, boys and girls? Is it a helicopter? Or maybe a tractor?'

The children ran to the window to look out.

'Nothing there, Mr Brown,' called the children.

Mr Brown looked at Tom. Tom hardly dared to breathe. Had Billy given himself away?

Then out of the corner of his eye Tom saw Mr Brown step down from the dais and begin to walk slowly towards him.

by Donna Gibbs

1. Why did Tom creep through the fence?
   - **A** It was a small space to get through.
   - **B** It was a game he liked playing.
   - **C** He didn't want his parents to hear him visiting the kittens.
   - **D** He wanted to frighten the kittens by arriving unexpectedly.

2. Billy liked
   - **A** hiding in Tom's jumper.
   - **B** rubbing his nose against Tom's leg.
   - **C** hiding in Tom's desk.
   - **D** being with the other kittens.

3. What makes you judge that the classroom is old-fashioned? Choose all that apply.
   - **A** The teacher writes with chalk on a blackboard.
   - **B** The children run to the window.
   - **C** The desk has an inkwell hole.
   - **D** The children work silently at their Maths.

4. The low vibratory sound Mr Brown heard nearby came from
   - **A** a passing helicopter.
   - **B** Billy's loud purring.
   - **C** a distant tractor.
   - **D** Tom's noisy breathing.

5. How did Tom feel when Mr Brown began to walk towards him?

   ....

   ....

   ....

   ....

   ....

   ....

Answers and explanations on p. 112

Mixed questions

Use the **Step-by-step guide** on page 4 to help you read the text and then answer the questions below. Circle the correct answers or write your answer on the lines.

Just in Time (Part 2)

'Whatever is that waving about on your desk, Tom?' asked Mr Brown as he stepped down from his dais.

Tom's heart sank. The cat he'd brought to school in secret, and hidden in his desk, was poking its tail out of the old inkwell hole!

'Nothing, Mr Brown,' he said, pushing the tail back in.

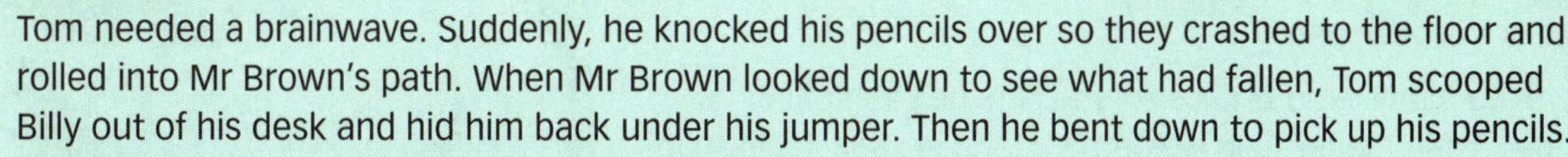

Billy thought this was a new game and pushed his tail up through the hole again. Mr Brown was walking slowly towards Tom's desk.

Tom needed a brainwave. Suddenly, he knocked his pencils over so they crashed to the floor and rolled into Mr Brown's path. When Mr Brown looked down to see what had fallen, Tom scooped Billy out of his desk and hid him back under his jumper. Then he bent down to pick up his pencils.

'Are you sure there's nothing in your desk, Tom?'

'Yes, Mr Brown,' said Tom.

'I see,' said Mr Brown, looking at the wriggling bump under Tom's jumper.

'Make sure there is nothing there after morning tea too, won't you Tom?' he said.

'Yes, Mr Brown,' Tom replied. Relief splashed all through him. His brainwave had saved him. Just in time!

by Donna Gibbs

1 *as he stepped down from his dais* *(line 3)*

The *dais* Mr Brown stepped down from is

- **A** a desk.
- **B** a low platform.
- **C** a throne.
- **D** a chair.

2 Billy *pushed his tail up through the hole again* *(lines 8–9)* because

- **A** he didn't find the hole the first time.
- **B** he thought it was time for some exercise.
- **C** he needed more space.
- **D** he thought he was playing a new game.

3 Which happened first?

- **A** Mr Brown asked Tom what was waving about on his desk.
- **B** Tom had a brainwave.
- **C** Tom got Billy out of the desk and under his jumper.
- **D** Billy waved his tail out of the inkwell hole.

4 Why did Tom drop his pencils?

- **A** to distract Mr Brown
- **B** to show off
- **C** to teach Billy to stop the game
- **D** to confuse Billy

5 What kind of teacher do you judge Mr Brown to be?

- **A** foolish and silly
- **B** firm but kind-hearted
- **C** strict and mean
- **D** crabby and unpleasant

6 What is another title you could give the story?

....

....

....

....

Answers and explanations on pp. 112–113

Mixed questions

Use the **Step-by-step guide** on page 4 to help you read the text and then answer the questions below. Circle the correct answers or write your answer on the lines.

First Nations Australian trackers

First Nations Australian trackers are famous for 'reading' the land as though it is telling them a story. Sometimes they spend hours in one spot scanning the ground for signs of the beginning of a track. When they look closely at size, depth and spacing of tracks they can tell how quickly a person or animal is moving, its gender and where it is heading.

Early explorers such as Major Mitchell and Edward John Eyre took First Nations trackers with them to act as guides through difficult country and to help them locate food and water. The success of these explorers owed much to the knowledge and skills of their companions.

There are many famous cases of trackers helping to find people lost in the bush. In western Victoria in 1864, locals had searched for more than a week for three lost children. When First Nations trackers joined the search they found them within a day. The leader of the trackers, Djungadjinganook, nicknamed King Richard, was later a member of the first Australian cricket team to tour England.

On many occasions First Nations trackers have helped locate criminals and bushrangers who were hiding out in rough country. A famous example of this is when they helped police capture Ned Kelly in the Victorian town of Glenrowan in 1880.

Source: Wikimedia Commons

1. How do First Australian trackers 'read' the land?
   - **A** by looking at their surroundings
   - **B** by scanning their surroundings
   - **C** by understanding the meanings of signs they see in their surroundings
   - **D** by telling people stories about the land

2. To find the beginning of a track, First Nations trackers sometimes
   - **A** work out where a track is heading.
   - **B** look closely at the size of a track.
   - **C** spend hours in one spot.
   - **D** use magical powers.

3. What was amazing about the First Nations trackers finding the children?
   - **A** They found them in only a day when they'd been lost for over a week.
   - **B** One of the trackers was an Australian cricketer.
   - **C** They surprised even themselves.
   - **D** They found all three children at the same time.

4. Which famous bushranger did the First Nations trackers help capture in 1880?
   - **A** Major Mitchell
   - **B** Ned Kelly
   - **C** Glenrowan
   - **D** Edward John Eyre

5. What are First Australian trackers famous for?

   ....

   ....

   ....

   ....

   ....

Answers and explanations on p. 113

Mixed questions

Use the **Step-by-step guide** on page 4 to help you read the text and then answer the questions below. Circle the correct answers or write your answer on the lines.

I remember

Homework for Year 3: Write down six of your memories from when you were younger. Write a sentence or two about each.

I remember:

- my first day at Kindy. The playground looked ENORMOUS. I followed the teacher everywhere. She smiled kindly at me and said I was like a duckling with its mother.
- when I fell off the jungle gym at school and broke my nose. Everyone crowded around me. I felt as if I was famous.
- my friend licking her ice-cream more slowly than I did. I finished mine and she was still licking hers. I decided I'd do that next time we were eating an ice-cream together. I forgot, but she didn't.
- wearing my new watch in the bath by mistake. It wasn't waterproof. Next morning I looked to see if it was still telling the time. It wasn't.
- when I had mumps. My glands got very swollen and my brother said the back of my head looked like a balloon. It gives me the giggles to think about it.
- getting a new, shiny scooter. I was allowed to ride to the end of the street. I pretended I was an ambulance and went really fast.

by Bindy

1 Bindy uses capital letters for the word *ENORMOUS* (line 5) because she

A likes the look of the capital letters.
B left the caps key on by mistake.
C wants to emphasise how big the playground looked.
D wants to attract everyone's attention.

2 The teacher describes Bindy as being like a duckling because

A Bindy follows her around.
B she wants to make fun of Bindy.
C she loves Bindy and she loves ducklings.
D she wants to make Bindy get out of her way.

3 What made Bindy feel famous?

A falling off the jungle gym
B everyone crowding around
C breaking her nose
D being at school

4 Bindy's watch stops working because

A it is waterproof. **B** it is faulty.
C it isn't waterproof. **D** it loses time.

5 Bindy went *really fast* (line 18) on her red scooter because

A she loved going fast.
B she was pretending to be an ambulance.
C she wanted to see how quickly it would go.
D she was showing her friends how quickly she could go.

6 What are Bindy's memories most often about?

....

....

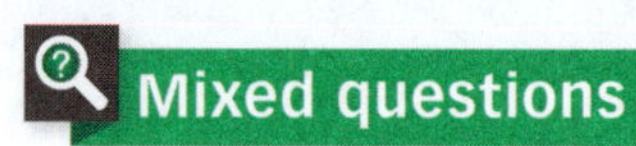

Mixed questions

Use the **Step-by-step guide** on page 4 to help you read the text and then answer the questions below. Circle the correct answers or write your answer on the lines.

Colours and their meanings

People connect colours with particular ideas, feelings and moods. The colour red, for example, is often connected with anger, danger and violence. You 'see red' when you are angry; on the other hand, red is the colour of love and is celebrated with red hearts and red roses.

Countries, schools and sporting teams use colours to represent themselves. Australia's national colours are green and gold like the wattle, its floral emblem. The green has links with Australia's gum trees, bush and pastures, and the gold with its beaches, deserts, mineral wealth and grain harvests.

Many idioms rely on connections that people make with colours. You can feel blue (sad), tickled pink (pleased) or eaten up with the green-eyed monster (jealous). The connections people make with colours also change. People often give newborns something blue for a boy or pink for a girl, but long ago in some cultures the opposite was common practice.

For Chinese people red symbolises good luck and happiness, whereas in South Africa it can be the colour of sadness and mourning. White is worn at weddings in the West but in some Eastern cultures the colour white has strong connections with death and funerals.

1. The colour red in the idiom '*see red*' *(line 3)* is linked with
   - **A** love.
   - **B** anger.
   - **C** the heart.
   - **D** romance.

2. The phrase *on the other hand* *(lines 3–4)* means
   - **A** however.
   - **B** also.
   - **C** in addition.
   - **D** as well.

3. National colours arouse people's connections with
   - **A** their own team's sporting achievements.
   - **B** their favourite colours.
   - **C** their country.
   - **D** their school.

4. The colour green in the phrase *the green-eyed monster* *(line 10)* is linked with
   - **A** grass.
   - **B** feeling sick.
   - **C** things that eat you.
   - **D** peace.

5. Which statements are true of colours and their meanings? Choose all that apply.
   - **A** Colours have fixed meanings.
   - **B** The meanings linked with colours can change over time.
   - **C** Colours mean different things in different cultures.
   - **D** Colours communicate meanings.

6. What connections does your favourite colour have for you?

   ....

   ....

   ....

   ....

Answers and explanations on p. 114

Mixed questions

Use the **Step-by-step guide** on page 4 to help you read the text and then answer the questions below. Circle the correct answers or write your answer on the lines.

The Indigenous Round

The twenty-first century has seen the number of First Nations Australian players in football teams increase rapidly. Their ball-handling skills and fast, skilful play on the field are becoming legendary.

In 2007 the AFL (Australian Football League) decided to devote a round of matches in the season to celebrate First Nations Australian culture and the contribution of Indigenous players to Australian Rules Football. Known as the Indigenous Round, this is now a regular highlight of the football season.

Entertainment before the matches of this round includes a traditional warrior dance, musical performances, a curtain-raiser between two First Nations football teams drawn from Australia and its territories, and a walk from Federation Square to the Melbourne Cricket Ground in support of reconciliation.

Teams wear special Indigenous jerseys for the match. The Hawks, for example, wear a jersey designed by a Wiradjuri painter that tells the story of the ancient lands that are now the Melbourne suburb of Hawthorn. 'We play with pride on Wurundjeri land' is printed on the back of each jersey.

1 *a round of matches* (line 8)

What is a *round*?

- **A** a circle
- **B** a series of games
- **C** a completed game
- **D** a song sung at the football

2 Hawks is the name of

- **A** a First Nations footballer.
- **B** an Australian football team.
- **C** a non-Indigenous footballer.
- **D** a First Nations football team.

3 What is the author's attitude towards the Indigenous Round?

- **A** disapproving
- **B** approving
- **C** concerned
- **D** uninterested

4 What is a *curtain-raiser* (line 15)?

- **A** a short game played before the main game
- **B** a game played only for fun
- **C** a short game that follows the main game
- **D** an unimportant game

5 Why do footballers wear Indigenous jerseys for the Indigenous Round?

....

....

....

....

Answers and explanations on pp. 114–115

Mixed questions

Use the **Step-by-step guide** on page 4 to help you read the text and answer the questions below. Circle the correct answers or write your answer on the lines.

Should weekend sport be compulsory?

Liz: I feel strongly that boys and girls should be made to play sport at weekends, particularly now we are surrounded by so much technology. Even primary school children spend lots of their time on phones and the internet. This means they don't get enough exercise.

Tchi: You need to make the choice for yourself though. That way you grow up looking after your own health. I think you should do exercise of some kind at the weekend but you shouldn't be made to do it by someone else.

Jem: Yes, I agree because that's sensible. But I'm not! I know I wouldn't play cricket or whatever at the weekends if it was my choice. So I see it as the rule you have to have.

Amy: I think maybe it could be compulsory for girls but definitely not for boys.

Jem: That's sexist, Amy. Why not boys?

Amy: They already do enough sport.

Liz: I don't think so. Have you met my brothers? They are permanently glued to their computers. Not a good look.

Teacher: Let's take a vote then. Who votes for compulsory sport at weekends? Two. Against? Two. Dead heat.

1 Who says you shouldn't be made to play sport?

A Liz **B** Tchi
C Jem **D** Amy

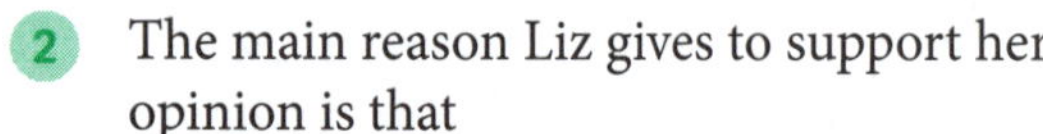

2 The main reason Liz gives to support her opinion is that

A her brothers don't exercise enough.
B boys and girls need time with technology.
C technology prevents children from getting enough exercise.
D you begin to look unhealthy.

3 *But I'm not!* (line 18)

When Jem says this, he means he's not

A in agreement with Tchi.
B sensible.
C in agreement with Liz.
D playing cricket.

4 Jem calls Amy's opinion *sexist* (line 25) because it is based on a person's

A attitude. **B** gender.
C character. **D** behaviour.

5 Who would have voted against compulsory weekend sport?

A Jem and Amy **B** Liz and Jem
C Tchi and Liz **D** Amy and Tchi

6 Whose opinion did you find most persuasive in this discussion? Give reasons for your choice.

....

....

....

....

Answers and explanations on p. 115

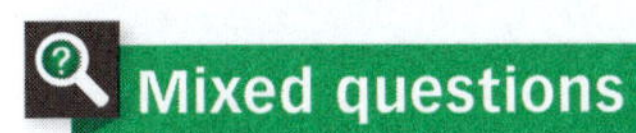

Mixed questions

Use the **Step-by-step guide** on page 4 to help you read the text and answer the questions below. Circle the correct answers or write your answer on the lines.

When I grow up

When I grow up
I plan to be
someone who lives
by the sea.

I'll sail my boat
and surf and swim
eat fish and chips
to suit my whim.

Perhaps to keep me
out of debt
I'd learn to fly
an airline jet.

I could act in a film,
or drive racing cars
or turn astronaut and
zoom to the stars.

I could be a cop
or a very brave firey
Or live on the land
and own my own dairy.

I'd milk the cows,
have a tractor to drive.
Shear the sheep,
get honey from a hive.

Mum says, 'You're dreaming,'
and she's quite right.
Yet it's half the fun
on a cold winter's night.

It's far in the future
so I really don't know.
But I *do* like dreaming
about it so!

1 The first plan the narrator mentions is to

A fly a plane.
B act in a film.
C sail a boat.
D live by the sea.

2 *out of debt* (line 11)

The word *debt* means

A having too much money.
B owing money.
C trouble.
D prison.

3 The mother's attitude towards her child's plans is

A disappointed.
B realistic.
C anxious.
D over excited.

4 The mood of the poem is

A cheerful.
B sad.
C heavy-hearted.
D dramatic.

5 The narrator chooses things to do that are mostly

A active.
B brave.
C useful.
D difficult.

6 What kind of personality does the narrator have?

....

....

....

Answers and explanations on pp. 115–116

Mixed questions

Use the **Step-by-step guide** on page 4 to help you read the text and answer the questions below. Circle the correct answers or write your answer on the lines.

Henry Lawson's bush school

Henry Lawson, the famous Australian author, attended a state primary school in the bush in Eurunderee, New South Wales, in the 1870s. His father, a Norwegian who had come to Australia in the gold rushes, built the school out of bark and made easels and blackboards from old wood to furnish it. The rest of the furniture came from second-hand cast-offs. The schoolmaster, John Tiernan, an Irishman, camped in a shelter attached to the school.

On Henry's first day, he was given copybooks, and pen and ink. The lesson books used were those published for the National Schools of Ireland. The Australian children often found the contents confusing, particularly those about geography. Mr Tiernan was worried that the school might blow over in a storm and wanted to have a plan in place. For this reason he gave the children a lot of practice at diving under their desks.

The pupils were a mixed bunch. Henry remembered a tomboy, a joker, a sneak, one always in trouble, another always wanting a fight and 'the rest in between'. He also recalled a black goanna. It used to lie in the classroom on a beam over the girls' seats. According to Henry the goanna liked to 'improve his mind a little, and doze a lot'.

1. Who built the old bush school?
   - **A** Henry Lawson
   - **B** Henry Lawson's father
   - **C** John Tiernan
   - **D** the government

2. Why did Mr Tiernan think the school might blow over?
   - **A** It was made out of bark.
   - **B** His 'home' was attached to it.
   - **C** It housed so many children.
   - **D** Irish schools often blew over.

3. Why are some of the words in this account in inverted commas?
   - **A** They are old-fashioned words.
   - **B** They are the author's words.
   - **C** They are used to emphasise what is said.
   - **D** They are things Henry Lawson has said.

4. Why would the children at the bush school have found their school books confusing?
   - **A** They were not very clever students.
   - **B** The school books were about Ireland and the northern hemisphere.
   - **C** They were written in Irish.
   - **D** They were very badly written.

5. *'improve his mind a little, and doze a lot'* *(line 20)*

   This is amusing because
   - **A** goannas like to sleep.
   - **B** it assumes the goanna is a pupil in the class.
   - **C** goannas would be afraid of the girls.
   - **D** you expect the goanna to be fierce.

6. How is the old bush school different from a bush school today?

   ....

   ....

   ....

   ....

   ....

Answers and explanations on pp. 116–117

Mixed questions

Use the **Step-by-step guide** on page 4 to help you read the text and answer the questions below. Circle the correct answers or write your answer on the lines.

Scene one

(the home of Mr and Mrs Rat, Portsmouth, England, 1788)

Mrs Rat: Well, we're packed and ready at last.

Mr Rat: Excellent, dear. Have you packed the seasick powders? You know how my stomach plays up on long sea voyages.

Mrs Rat: There's no room in the case. We'll be on the ship for several months. You'll get used to it.

Mr Rat: Perhaps Harold's case has a wee spot?

Mrs Rat: Well, Arthur, you can ask him. Here he comes now. Oh dear, I wish he wouldn't skate on those new-fangled roller-blades.

Harold: (*sliding to a sudden halt*) Hi Mum. Hi Dad. Did you see me do that jump over the rubbish bin? Wheeee! Great fun.

Mr Rat: Yes, dear. Remarkable. (*in a pleading tone of voice*) You wouldn't have a tiny bit of space in your case for my seasick powders would you?

Harold: Sorry Dad. No space. It's bulging.

Mrs Rat: What's it bulging with, Harold?

Harold: Just a few things for the voyage.

Mrs Rat: What things, Harold?

Harold: Camemberts, bries—that sort of thing. Picked them up from the shop this morning.

Mrs Rat: Well, that's alright then.

(*a carriage draws to a halt*)

Here's our carriage, Arthur. Leave those rollerblades behind, Harold. That's one thing we're not taking to Australia!

1 The rats are preparing for

- **A** an outing in a dinghy.
- **B** a carriage ride.
- **C** a road trip.
- **D** a sea voyage.

2 Mrs Rat is a character who is

- **A** soft hearted and sympathetic.
- **B** firm minded and tough.
- **C** considerate and generous.
- **D** weak and feeble.

3 Mrs Rat calls Harold's rollerblades *new-fangled* (line 16) to express her

- **A** admiration.
- **B** approval.
- **C** disapproval.
- **D** horror.

4 A title for this scene could be

- **A** Lost.
- **B** The voyage.
- **C** Three blind rats.
- **D** Preparing for departure.

5 You can tell this is a play script, rather than another kind of text, because

- **A** it includes humour.
- **B** it includes several characters.
- **C** it includes stage directions.
- **D** it has a plot.

6 Do you think Harold will leave the rollerblades behind? Explain.

....

....

....

....

Answers and explanations on p. 117

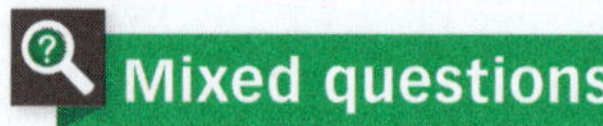

Mixed questions

Use the **Step-by-step guide** on page 4 to help you read the text and answer the questions below. Circle the correct answers or write your answer on the lines.

Caught

Text 1

'Will you walk into my parlour?' said the Spider to the Fly,
'Tis the prettiest little parlour that ever you did spy;
The way into my parlour is up a winding stair,
And I've a many curious things to shew when you are there.'
'Oh no, no,' said the little Fly, 'to ask me is in vain,
For who goes up your winding stair
can ne'er come down again.'

by Mary Howitt, 1829

Text 2

Web-building spiders make webs as an efficient way to catch their food. They make a silken liquid in glands in their abdomens for this purpose. The spider squeezes the liquid out through tiny holes in its body and as it meets the air it forms a fine, tough thread that is much finer than a human hair. The glands produce sticky silk to trap the spider's prey and non-sticky silk to make the spokes and centre of the web.

Scientists say that spiders' silk, although very fine, is also very strong. It is strong enough, for example, to catch a bee travelling at 32 kilometres per hour without breaking. In the future spider's silk may be farmed for manufacturing a range of products.

1 You would find the first text in a
- **A** book of plays.
- **B** newspaper.
- **C** book of poetry.
- **D** science textbook.

2 You would find the second text in a
- **A** book of plays.
- **B** newspaper.
- **C** book of poetry.
- **D** science textbook.

3 The spider in Text 1 talks about its web as though it were
- **A** its own body.
- **B** a person's home with stairs and a room for guests.
- **C** a museum.
- **D** a home for stray insects.

4 Why does the fly in Text 1 refuse the spider's invitation?
- **A** It has already had breakfast.
- **B** It has too much else to do.
- **C** It knows the spider will trap and eat it.
- **D** It finds climbing stairs difficult.

5 The silk spun by spiders is
- **A** fine and strong.
- **B** fine and fragile.
- **C** tough and thick.
- **D** fragile and flimsy.

6 Why don't spiders get trapped in their own webs?

....

....

....

....

....

Answers and explanations on pp. 117–118

Mixed questions

Use the **Step-by-step guide** on page 4 to help you read the text and answer the questions below. Circle the correct answers or write your answer on the lines.

Safe cycling

Portsea Primary's Weekly Newsletter

This week our whole class took part in a bike education program. We went to a special place owned by the police. It was set up like a real city with pavements, gutters, curbs and mini traffic lights.

There were classes by different instructors. The first one told us about bike helmets. We practised fitting the helmet and doing it up correctly. Our instructor said wearing a helmet can reduce the risk of head injury by between 60 and 90%. I'm always going to wear mine in future.

Then came the best part. We rode our cycles on the pavement and then later on the roads, where we had to stop at the mini traffic lights. We practised riding in a straight line, braking correctly and turning corners safely. No-one fell off but one of us nearly did.

In the afternoon we learned how to look after our bikes so they work properly. We were shown how to check our tyres and other parts of the bike. We also learned how to lubricate the bike's chains and cables.

I would highly recommend this program to everyone who has the opportunity to do it. Safe cycling!

Jess, Year 3

1 The first class of the program was about bike

A tyres. **B** chains.
C helmets. **D** brakes.

2 *Helmets need a Standards Australia mark on them to show they are approved.*

To which paragraph could you add this sentence?

A paragraph one
B paragraph two
C paragraph three
D paragraph four

3 *mini traffic lights* (line 17)

The word *mini* means

A a larger version.
B a game version.
C a miniature version.
D a middle-sized version.

4 Jess's attitude to the bike education program is

A enthusiastic.
B critical.
C amused.
D disappointed.

5 How was the bike program helpful for Jess?

....

....

....

....

....

Answers and explanations on p. 118

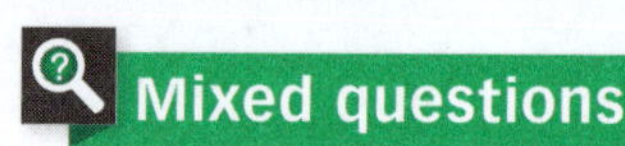

Mixed questions

Use the **Step-by-step guide** on page 4 to help you read the text and answer the questions below. Circle the correct answers or write your answer on the lines.

My Shadow

I have a little shadow that goes in and out with me,
And what can be the use of him is more than I can see,
He is very, very like me from the heels up to the head;
And I see him jump before me, when I jump into my bed.

The funniest thing about him is the way he likes to grow
—Not at all like proper children, which is always very slow;
For he sometimes shoots up taller like an india-rubber ball,
And he sometimes gets so little that there's none of him at all.

He hasn't got a notion of how children ought to play,
And can only make a fool of me in every sort of way.
He stays so close beside me, he's a coward you can see;
I'd think shame to stick to nursie as that shadow sticks to me!

One morning, very early, before the sun was up,
I rose and found the shining dew on every buttercup;
But my lazy little shadow, like an arrant sleepy-head,
Had stayed at home behind me and was fast asleep in bed.

by Robert Louis Stevenson, 1885

1 The narrator is

A a teenager.
B a young boy.
C a young girl.
D an adult.

2 Why does the narrator compare the shadow to an india-rubber ball?

A It is small and round.
B It comes from India.
C It can shoot high in the air.
D It is fun to play with.

3 *He hasn't got a notion of how children ought to play* (line 10)

The modal words *ought to* mean

A should.
B could.
C would.
D do.

4 What is funny about the way little shadow grows?

A He grows very slowly.
B He can change size quite quickly.
C He doesn't grow at all.
D He copies the way children grow.

5 The narrator would NOT describe the little shadow as

A useless. **B** cowardly.
C lazy. **D** independent.

6 *But my lazy little shadow … / … was fast asleep in bed.* (lines 16–17)

What is the real reason that the little shadow isn't with the narrator?

....

....

....

Answers and explanations on pp. 118–119

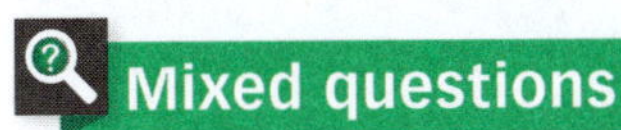

Mixed questions

Use the **Step-by-step guide** on page 4 to help you read the text and answer the questions below. Circle the correct answers or write your answer on the lines.

Australian inventors

My name is Phoebe. I am in Year Five. In my view Australian inventors are often overlooked and are mostly unknown by today's young people. Let me prove my point.

How many of you have heard of Donald Bradman? Mmm. That's 18 out of 25.

How many have heard of Nicole Kidman? 20 out of 25.

That's quite a high proportion. The reason that the Don and Nic are so well known is that the media is always highlighting the achievements of sports people and celebrities. But how often do you get to hear about Australia's very own inventors who change people's lives with what they achieve?

Have you heard of Graeme Clark? 3 out of 25. The amazing bionic ear was his achievement.

Fiona Wood? 5 out of 25. She invented a spray-on skin technique for burns victims.

There are hundreds of other things invented by Australians such as the woomera, the stump jump plough, the motor mower, the black box flight recorder, Google maps, Wifi technology, the scramjet, the heg and many more. I'm not going to tell you about these intriguing inventions. I just hope you'll get interested in Australian inventors and want to find out for yourselves.

Thanks for listening, Year 3.

1 When Phoebe asks questions, the members of the audience reply by

- **A** taking no notice.
- **B** raising a hand if they recognise the name.
- **C** calling out a reply.
- **D** raising a hand if they don't recognise the name.

2 *That's quite a high proportion.* *(line 6)*

Phoebe says this to try to show that young people

- **A** know a lot about sports people.
- **B** listen carefully to what is said.
- **C** are not interested in what the media reports.
- **D** know a lot about sports people and celebrities.

3 Phoebe uses the names *the Don* and *Nic* *(line 6)* to

- **A** reinforce her point that they are well known.
- **B** cause confusion.
- **C** imply she is on friendly terms with them.
- **D** impress her audience.

4 Phoebe doesn't describe the inventions she lists because she

- **A** doesn't know what they are.
- **B** wants to arouse the curiosity and interest of the audience.
- **C** likes being mysterious.
- **D** hopes someone will call out an explanation.

5 This text is the transcript of a

- **A** live conversation.
- **B** live speech.
- **C** class discussion.
- **D** TV advertisement.

6 Do you find Phoebe's arguments convincing? Explain your reasons.

....

....

....

....

Answers and explanations on p. 119

Mixed questions

Use the **Step-by-step guide** on page 4 to help you read the text and answer the questions below. Circle the correct answers or write your answer on the lines.

Brr Brrr. Brr Brrr.

Gran: Hi Tommy. What's your news?

Tommy: Hi Gran. Not much. I'm trying to persuade mum to let me do a paper round to save up for a guitar.

Gran: What does she say?

Tommy: She says I have to wait until I'm eleven as it's not legal until then.

Gran: Well, that's not long to wait.

Tommy: S'pose not.

Gran: My first job was in a toy shop on Saturdays. I wanted to save up for a miniature musical box that I desperately wanted.

Tommy: Did you get it?

Gran: I did and I kept it on my windowsill. I've still got it.

Tommy: What was it like working in a toy shop? How old were you?

Gran: I was twelve and I loved it. The shop had plenty of toys and also a doll hospital where children could leave their dolls to be mended. It was 1956. I remember because the Melbourne Olympic Games were showing on a television in the cafe next door.

Tommy: Did it take you long to save up?

Gran: It seemed like forever. But I got there in the end. You will too.

Tommy: Guess so. See you, Gran.

Gran: Bye Tommy.

1 Gran was born in

A 1956. **B** 1944.
C Melbourne. **D** Athens.

2 Tommy and Gran have a relationship that is

A difficult. **B** comfortable.
C hostile. **D** awkward.

3 *What does she say?* (line 5)

Tommy's gran asks Tommy this because she

A likes to snoop.
B is being careful not to interfere between Tommy and his mother.
C can't think of anything else to say.
D is a stickybeak.

4 *a miniature musical box* (line 11)

What does the adjective *miniature* mean?

A average sized **B** large
C very tiny **D** big

5 What was unusual about the toy shop where Gran worked?

A It was in Melbourne.
B It had plenty of toys.
C There was a television in the shop next door.
D It had a doll hospital attached to it.

6 Would Tommy feel encouraged by this conversation with his Gran? Explain your reasons.

....

....

....

....

Answers and explanations on p. 120

Mixed questions

Use the **Step-by-step guide** on page 4 to help you read the text and answer the questions below. Circle the correct answers or write your answer on the lines.

The Wombat

The Wombat (or, as it is called by the natives of Port Jackson, the Womback) is a squat, thick, short-legged, and rather inactive quadruped.

…

This animal has not any claim to swiftness of foot, as most men could run it down. Its pace is hobbling or shuffling, something like the awkward gait of a bear. In disposition it is mild and gentle, as becomes a grass-eater; but it bites hard, and is furious when provoked. Mr. Bass* never heard its voice but at that time; it was a low cry, between a hissing and a whizzing, which could not be heard at a distance of more than thirty or forty yards. He chased one, and with his hands under his belly suddenly lifted him off the ground without hurting him, and laid him upon his back along his arm, like a child. It made no noise, nor any effort to escape, not even a struggle. Its countenance was placid and undisturbed, and it seemed as contented as if it had been nursed by Mr. Bass from its infancy. He carried the beast upwards of a mile, and often shifted him from arm to arm, sometimes laying him upon his shoulder …

Extract from *An Account of the English Colony in New South Wales* by David Collins, 1804

*George Bass, the English navigator and explorer

1. Which word in the text tells you how many feet a wombat has?
   - **A** short-legged
   - **B** quadruped
   - **C** gait
   - **D** countenance

2. *Womback* (*line 3*) is
   - **A** a British word.
   - **B** a made-up word.
   - **C** a First Nations word.
   - **D** a word used by Mr Bass.

3. Mr Bass was able to catch a wombat because
   - **A** he was a very swift runner.
   - **B** it didn't move at a fast pace.
   - **C** it liked being carried.
   - **D** he had a lot of practice catching wombats.

4. The author suggests that wombats are
   - **A** nasty and cruel.
   - **B** extremely lazy and slothful.
   - **C** even-tempered unless aroused.
   - **D** very timid.

5. To what is the wombat compared by the author? Choose all that apply.
   - **A** a child
   - **B** a nurse
   - **C** a bear
   - **D** a grass-eater

6. Why does the author give measurements in yards rather than metres?

   ....

   ....

   ....

   ....

   ....

Answers and explanations on pp. 120–121

ANSWERS

Fact-finding questions

Counting (page 28)

1 A **2** D **3** B **4** B **5** See below

Explanations

1 **A** is correct. This is a **fact-finding** question. The answer is stated directly in the text. You read *When I was one / I had lots of fun* (see lines 2–3). **B**, **C** and **D** are incorrect as they are ages where Tilly doesn't refer to having lots of fun.

2 **D** is correct. This is a **fact-finding** question. The answer is stated directly in the text. You read *Eight. Have you guessed? / I like it the best* (see lines 12–13). **A**, **B** and **C** are incorrect as they are not ages Tilly says she likes best.

3 **B** is correct. This is a **fact-finding** question. The answer is stated directly in the text. Tilly talks about the things she likes about being eight but says *I do have some doubts / about turning nine* (see lines 18–19). This means she hasn't turned nine yet. **A**, **C** and **D** are incorrect as they are not the age Tilly is now.

4 **B** is correct. This is a **fact-finding** question. The answer is stated directly in the text. The thought Tilly has that gives her some doubts is *Will the big kids be mean?* (see line 20). This means she wonders if the older children might be mean to her when she turns nine. **A** is incorrect as Tilly hardly ever worries about anything. **C** is incorrect as there is no evidence that Tilly is afraid of growing up. **D** is incorrect as Tilly has some doubts about what it will be like to be nine but she decides *It's sure to be fine* (see line 21). This is different from never wanting to be nine.

5 This is a **fact-finding** question. The answer is stated directly in the text. Tilly says life may seem good to her because she is *easy to please* (see line 23). She also thinks her happy attitude might be because life is a really good thing to be part of—it's *the bee's knees* (see line 25).

Where to get your new pet (page 29)

1 B and D **2** B **3** A **4** C **5** See below

Explanations

1 **B** and **D** are correct. This is a **fact-finding** question. The answer is stated directly in the text. You read *I think people should get their pets from animal shelters or pet rescue groups* (see lines 3–4). **A** and **C** are incorrect because they name places and people Ari thinks you should not get your pet from.

2 **B** is correct. This is a **fact-finding** question. The answer is stated directly in the text. You read *The money used to pay to adopt your pet helps fund these organisations* (see lines 6–7). Your money helps fund the animal shelter. **A** is incorrect because animal shelters or pet-rescue groups don't use the money to *only* cover the cost of vaccinations—they use it in various ways to help fund the shelter, including paying for vaccinations. **C** is incorrect as volunteers give their services for free and are not paid by these organisations. **D** is incorrect as these organisations rescue homeless animals—they don't buy them.

3 **A** is correct. This is a **fact-finding** question. The answer is stated directly in the text. You read *Some shelters even have programs to match the personality of a pet with that of its new owner. 'Meet Your Match' is a program I tried and that's how I found Ruffie* (see lines 10–12). *'Meet Your Match'* is a program about matching a pet's personality with that of its new owner's. **B**, **C** and **D** are incorrect because *'Meet your Match'* is not a program about finding a pet that is healthy, matching people with work that suits them or matching pets with each other.

4 **C** is correct. This is a **fact-finding** question. You read *shelter animals cost less than animals*

from breeders or pet shops (see line 18). They are less expensive than animals bought from pet shops. **A** is incorrect as you read that they cost less, not more, than animals bought from pet shops. **B** is incorrect because you read that they cost less than animals bought from breeders, not the same amount. **D** is incorrect because you read that shelter animals cost less than those from other places, not twice their price.

5 This is a **fact-finding** question. Ari thinks you should try to find your pet from an animal shelter or a rescue group before you look elsewhere.

Famous explorers: Bass and Flinders (page 30)

1 B **2** C **3** C **4** A **5** See below

Explanations

1 **B** is correct. This is a **fact-finding** question. The answer is stated directly in the text. You read *Matthew Flinders read the adventure story, Robinson Crusoe* (see lines 2–3). **A**, **C** and **D** are incorrect as *Robinson Crusoe* is not a boat, a real person or a place in England.

2 **C** is correct. This is a **fact-finding** question. The answer is stated directly in the text. You read *In 1795 Flinders, aged 21, sailed from England to Sydney on HMS* Reliance (see lines 7–8) and *On board, he met with George Bass* (see line 9). **A** and **D** are incorrect because they are dates from the years after Bass and Flinders arrived in Sydney. **B** is incorrect because neither Bass nor Flinders were born then.

3 **C** is correct. This is a **fact-finding** question. The answer is stated directly in the text. You read *they sailed … on the* Norfolk, *a ship built by convicts on Norfolk Island* (see lines 18–19). **A** and **B** are incorrect as neither Bass nor Flinders were ship builders. **D** is incorrect as the *Tom Thumb* is a rowing boat, not a builder.

4 **A** is correct. This is a **fact-finding** question. The answer is stated directly in the text. You read *Between 1802 and 1803 Flinders circumnavigated Australia on the* Investigator (see line 22). **B**, **C** and **D** are incorrect as Flinders did not circumnavigate the George's River or London. **D** is incorrect because Van Diemen's Land was circumnavigated earlier than 1802 by Bass and Flinders together.

5 This is a **fact-finding** question. The answer is stated directly in the text. The discovery was important because sailing time was saved on long journeys as ships no longer had to sail all the way around Tasmania—they could take a shorter route through Bass Strait.

How to throw a boomerang (page 31)

1 B **2** C **3** B **4** D **5** See below

Explanations

1 **B** is correct. This is a **fact-finding** question. The answer is stated directly in the text. You read *A boomerang is a curved piece of material, usually wood* (see line 2). **A** is incorrect because, although boomerangs can be made of plastic, this is not what they are usually made from. **C** is incorrect because boomerangs are not made from stone. **D** is incorrect as the material normally used to make a boomerang is wood, not fabric.

2 **C** is correct. This is a **fact-finding** question. The answer is stated directly in the text. You read *its V point or elbow* (see line 14). The *elbow* is another way of referring to *the V point*. **A**, **B** and **D** are incorrect because they name places that are not where the V point is on the boomerang.

3 **B** is correct. This is a **fact-finding** question. The answer is stated directly in the text. You read *The flat side should be against the palm of your hand* (see lines 15–16). This means you place the palm of your hand on the flat side of the boomerang. **A**, **C** and **D** are incorrect because the parts of the boomerang they name are not where you should place the palm of your hand before you throw it.

4 **D** is correct. This is a **fact-finding** question. The answer is stated directly in the text. You read *throw the boomerang as though you are casting a fishing line* (see lines 21–22). (You may realise that this will help it to spin.) **A** is incorrect because you are told to throw it like casting a fishing line, not like throwing a ball. **B** is incorrect because you are told to throw it in plenty of space and not where it will be trapped. **C** is incorrect because you are told to stand at a slight angle to the wind, not directly facing into it.

5 This is a **fact-finding** question. The answer is stated directly in the text. The reason you keep your eyes on the boomerang is so you can move to the right place to catch it.

Synthesis questions

How to make Anzac biscuits (page 36)

1 C **2** A **3** C **4** D **5** See below

Explanations

1 **C** is correct. This is a **synthesis** question. Paragraph one is not part of the recipe itself. It tells you about who the biscuits were originally made for and why there were no eggs included in it; in other words it gives background information. **A** is incorrect because the paragraph is longer, rather than shorter, than the other paragraphs. **B** and **D** are incorrect because paragraph one doesn't give any instructions about making biscuits.

2 **A** is correct. This is a **synthesis** question. The list names the ingredients you need to use to cook the recipe. **B** and **C** are incorrect because the list is a mixture of both dry and wet ingredients. **D** is incorrect because ingredients are listed, not utensils.

3 **C** is correct. This is a **synthesis** question. A list of the utensils you will use would be helpful as you could check you have them available before you begin cooking. **A** is incorrect because information about ANZAC Day would not help in any way with making the recipe. **B** and **D** are incorrect as the information is not directly related to the making of ANZAC biscuits.

4 **D** is correct. This is a **synthesis** question. The recipe omits the relevant information about how many biscuits you can expect to make. **A** and **B** are incorrect because paragraph one includes this information. **C** is incorrect because the list of ingredients states you can use *2 cups rolled oats or wheat bran* (see line 10).

5 This is a **synthesis** question. The best place to add this sentence is at the end of paragraph one. This is because paragraph one includes information that is not directly related to the making of ANZAC biscuits. If choc chips were added it would change the recipe and you wouldn't be making ANZAC biscuits. Another possible place is at the end of the list of ingredients since choc chips are an ingredient. They are not, however, an ingredient that you need to make ANZAC biscuits so this is a less suitable place.

Can I have a worm farm, please? (page 37)

1 B **2** C **3** A **4** A and D **5** See below

Explanations

1 **B** is correct. This is a **synthesis** question. Marietta says she wants to make the worm farm from foam boxes. She needs her Mum to buy the worms and a tap for her so she can complete it. **A** is incorrect because, although Marietta's mother thinks that is what Marietta wants, she learns Marietta doesn't expect her to buy a ready-made worm farm. **C** is incorrect because, although Marietta says her mum can use fertiliser on her vegetables if she gets a worm farm, that is not what she is trying to persuade her to do. **D** is incorrect because Marietta wants to do the composting herself with her worm farm.

2 **C** is correct. This is a **synthesis** question. Marietta says vegetables will grow better if you add fertiliser from the worm farm but she does not say that the vegetables will be free. **A**, **B** and **D** are incorrect. They are all put forward as arguments for Marietta having a worm farm. You read *they make liquid fertiliser to use on our vegetables* (**A**) (see line 9). You read *think how much rubbish won't have to be collected and how much landfill won't be used* (**B** and **D**) (see lines 12–13).

3 **A** is correct. This is a **synthesis** question. Marietta plans to make her own worm farm from free boxes. That way the cost will be kept low as only worms and a tap will need to be purchased. **B**, **C** and **D** are incorrect because Marietta does not mention saving her pocket money, her mum saving money or selling fertiliser to her friends.

4 **A** and **D** are correct. This is a **synthesis** question. **A** and **D** describe other advantages of having a worm farm. Marietta could have included these points to support her request. Reducing greenhouse gases is another benefit of having a worm farm (**A**). Worms do most

of the work so that makes looking after a worm farm easier (**D**). **B** is incorrect because knowing it is unwise to transfer compost worms to garden soil does not provide support for Marietta's request. **C** is incorrect. That everyone else has a worm farm is not a reason for Marietta having or not having a worm farm. Saying this would not have helped her to persuade her mother.

5 This is a **synthesis** question. Marietta's mother decides to agree to her having a worm farm when she realises how carefully Marietta has researched every single thing she needs to know about her project.

Doctor Dolittle (page 38)

1 B **2** A **3** C **4** A, B and C
5 See below

Explanations

1 **B** is correct. This is a **synthesis** question. The conversation is between Tommy Stubbins and Polynesia. No-one else speaks in this part of the text. **A** is incorrect because Tommy Stubbins's father doesn't speak in the text. **C** and **D** are incorrect because they name Dr Dolittle, whose name appears only in the title of the text.

2 **A** is correct. This is a **synthesis** question. You read *"Do you think I would ever be able to learn the language of the animals?" [asked Tommy Stubbins]* (see lines 2–3). The rest of the conversation is about working out an answer to Tommy's question. **B** is incorrect because Tommy's cleverness is not the main topic of the conversation. **C** is incorrect because, although the powers of observation are discussed, they are only part of the conversation. **D** is incorrect because the conversation is about whether Tommy could ever learn animal language, not whether Polynesia could teach it to Tommy.

3 **C** is correct. This is a **synthesis** question. Tommy says he doesn't know if he's clever at lessons and Polynesia says *"I don't suppose you have really missed much — to judge from what I have seen of school-boys"* (see lines 9–11). This means Polynesia thinks being clever at school is less important than noticing, comparing and observing things when learning animal language. **A**, **B** and **D** are incorrect because they name things that Polynesia says are very important when learning animal language.

4 **A**, **B** and **C** are correct. This is a **synthesis** question. There is nothing in the text about what made Tommy's family poor, Dr Dolittle's voyages or Polynesia's family background. **D** is incorrect because information about the powers of observation is included in the text in the last paragraph.

5 This is a **synthesis** question. Polynesia thinks the main thing you need to do to learn animal language is to notice small things about birds and animals such as how they move and behave.

Bunyips (page 39)

1 B **2** A **3** D **4** B **5** See below

Explanations

1 **B** is correct. This is a **synthesis** question. The text gives information about the role bunyips have in Australian folklore—who has seen them, which stories they are a part of, how they are thought to behave and what people think they look like. **A** is incorrect because the text is not about Australian folklore in general but about the bunyip's role in Australian folklore. **C** is incorrect because, while the text does include descriptions of bunyips, it does more than simply describe them. **D** is incorrect because, while the text says that the bunyip appears in Dreamtime stories, it also gives more general information about the role of the bunyip in Australian folklore.

2 **A** is correct. This is a **synthesis** question. Paragraph two reports on two separate pieces of evidence that people thought might prove the existence of bunyips. **B** is incorrect because the information given is not from the point of view of the bunyip so the reader does not know what adventures they might have had. **C** is incorrect because, although there is one suggestion about what a bunyip looks like in this paragraph, it is mostly about possible evidence that bunyips exist. **D** is incorrect because the bunyip's habits are not described in this paragraph.

3 **D** is correct. This is a **synthesis** question. The bunyip appeared on postage stamps in 1994. This comes after the 1847 skull was put on display, after the 1846 sighting was reported and long after Dreamtime stories. **A**, **B** and **C** are all incorrect as they happened before the series of postage stamps was published in 1994.

4 **B** is correct. This is a **synthesis** question. Although people think they have seen bunyips and they are part of Australian folklore, their existence has not yet been proved scientifically. **A**, **C** and **D** are incorrect because these statements are all true of bunyips.

5 This is a **synthesis** question. You read *No two bunyips ever seem to look the same* *(see line 19)*. There is variety in how people have described them. A bunyip might look like a large platypus (as in the sighting in paragraph two) or it may be *hairy and large, have red eyes* and *trail weeds* (as in paragraph three) *(see lines 19–20)*. You may have your own idea of a bunyip's appearance.

Inferring questions

Tell me about Tokyo (page 44)

1 B **2** D **3** A, B, C and D **4** B and C
5 See below

Explanations

1 **B** is correct. This is an **inferring** question. Elly and Akihito are email buddies who exchange messages by email on their electronic devices. **A**, **C** and **D** are incorrect because email buddies do not exchange messages using a pen, the telephone or the post.

2 **D** is correct. This is an **inferring** question. Elly lives on a small island off the mainland of Australia, whereas Akihito lives in Tokyo, a busy capital city in Japan. **A** is incorrect because neither Elly nor Akihito are only children—they both have siblings. **B** is incorrect because both Elly and Akihito go to school. **C** is incorrect because both Elly and Akihito live with their families.

3 **A**, **B**, **C** and **D** are correct. This is an **inferring** question. You can infer that Akihito's life is different from Elly's because her long school holidays are in January, she does not have earthquake drills, her hobby is fishing and she lives in a big house.

4 **B** and **C** are correct. This is an **inferring** question. You read *Tokyo is a very busy city with more than 13 million people* *(see lines 19–21)*and *trains take you everywhere you want to go* *(see lines 22–23)*. You can infer that driving a car in crowded Tokyo streets would be difficult and that since trains take you everywhere you would not need a car. **A** and **D** are incorrect because there is no evidence that Akihito's family is unable to afford a car or that their car was towed away.

5 This is an **inferring** question. You can infer that Akihito always follows the Japanese custom or tradition of taking off his shoes before he enters a home or a classroom.

How the birds got their colours (page 45)

1 B **2** C **3** A **4** D **5** See below

Explanations

1 **B** is correct. This is an **inferring** question. The bird tribes immediately went to help Dove when they heard her cry and they tried hard to help her get better. **A**, **C** and **D** are incorrect as there is no evidence that the bird tribes were unkind, or ignored or spread rumours about each other.

2 **C** is correct. This is an **inferring** question. You read *He didn't like everyone fussing around her instead of paying attention to him* *(see lines 13–14)*. You can infer from this that Crow was jealous of the attention Dove was getting. **A** is incorrect. There is no evidence that Crow always disliked Dove. **B** is incorrect because while Crow may have thought Dove was going to die this was not the reason he *glowered darkly* *(see line 13)* at her. **D** is incorrect because in this story Crow is nasty about Dove but there is no evidence he was nasty about everyone.

3 **A** is correct. This is an **inferring** question. All the birds except for Crow helped Dove, but it was Galah's idea to pierce the swelling on Dove's foot that really saved her life. **B** is incorrect as Crow did nothing at all to help. **C** and **D** are incorrect because, although they helped save Dove's life, they were not responsible for the action that healed her swollen foot.

4 **D** is correct. This is an **inferring** question. You read *Dove's colour drained away, leaving her pale and softly mottled* (see line 21). You can infer that her black colour drained away and faded to a light, pale colour —the colour many doves are today. **A** is incorrect because it was Lorikeet that received many of the rainbow's bright colours, not Dove. **B** is incorrect because Dove's black colouring drained from her and she became a pale, light colour. **C** is incorrect because it was Magpie that was splashed with white, not Dove.

5 This is an **inferring** question. Crow had been chased away from the circle of birds around Dove so he was out of range of the splashing colours. Crow stayed his original colour and nothing since has happened to change it.

Should school uniforms be compulsory? (page 46)

1 B **2** A and C **3** B **4** A **5** See below

Explanations

1 **B** is correct. This is an **inferring** question. You can infer that they listen to each other because the students often comment on what someone has just said. **A** is incorrect because expressing different opinions doesn't mean they have listened to what anyone else has said. **C** is incorrect because students sometimes agree with what has just been said. **D** is incorrect because acting politely does not prove you have listened to what someone says.

2 **A** and **C** are correct. This is an **inferring** question. Harry says *Wearing a uniform makes me feel locked up inside so I can't be me* (see line 21) and Jack says *Why should we have to wear them if we don't want to?* (see lines 16–17). These comments imply support for the idea that uniforms should not be compulsory. **B** is incorrect as Peta says nothing that suggests she is opposed to wearing a uniform. **D** is incorrect as Carey would prefer uniforms to be compulsory.

3 **B** is correct. This is an **inferring** question. Mina begins by being in favour of having a school uniform and shifts to the view that having a choice would be better. **A**, **C** and **D** are incorrect because neither Harry, Jack nor Carey change their point of view.

4 **A** is correct. This is an **inferring** question. You infer that the reason Peta quotes her friend is to show that wearing everyday clothes doesn't necessarily mean you have to worry every day. **B** and **D** are incorrect because Peta says this in response to what Carey has said. There is no suggestion she wants to show off or imply she is wiser than everybody else. **C** is incorrect because Peta is putting a different point of view about what it is like to wear everyday clothes to school, not saying Carey is wrong in her view about uniforms.

5 This is an **inferring** question. Peta supports Mina to try to bring the discussion to a close. She doesn't want to stay stuck in an argument that goes round and round—she wants to move forward.

Whodunnit? (page 47)

1 D **2** C **3** A, B, D **4** B **5** See below

Explanations

1 **D** is correct. This is an **inferring** question. You can infer that Woof is a dog because it has paws and because its name is the noise a dog makes when it barks. **A**, **B** and **C** are incorrect as giraffes, babies and budgerigars do not have paws.

2 **C** is correct. This is an **inferring** question. You can infer that Thomas doesn't believe in Martians and he knows Izzy doesn't either. He says *Yes, for sure!* (see line 7) in a jokey, almost sarcastic way. **A**, **B** and **D** are incorrect because Thomas knows Martians are not the explanation.

3 **A**, **B** and **D** are correct. This is an **inferring** question. Bandicoots have sharp claws that would allow them to make holes and dig out soil from the lawn. Their long pointy noses could be used to forage for food in the ground. Their looking for food at night is another reason to suspect them as no-one sees them in the day. **C** is incorrect because being like big mice is not a reason to think they might be digging holes in the lawn.

4 **B** is correct. This is an **inferring** question. There were new holes in the lawn and so it is very likely that the bandicoots came and dug the holes when the children were asleep. **A** and **D** are incorrect as invisible things could not have dug holes in the grass. **C** is incorrect as

there were new holes, meaning the bandicoots had been back.

5 This is an **inferring** question. You can infer that they are brother and sister because:
- they live in the same house (e.g. Thomas talks about *our lawn*) *(see lines 4–5)*
- they have the same parents. (e.g. Izzy says *Let's ask Mum and Dad*) *(see lines 28–29)*
- Thomas is a boy's name and Izzy (short for Isabella) is a girl's name.

Which did you choose? (page 48)

1 B **2** C **3** B **4** A and C **5** D
6 See below

Explanations

1 **B** is correct. This is an **inferring** question. You read *It took me ages to think of any I like! I read chapter books all the time now (see lines 4–5)*. You can infer that Pablo hasn't read any picture books for quite some time as now he reads chapter books. **A** is incorrect. Pablo has trouble remembering a favourite picture book but this does not prove he has a very bad memory in general. **C** is incorrect because there is no evidence that Pablo has given his picture books to his brother. **D** is incorrect because it is implied that he has read some picture books in the past and we know he has read *The Two Bullies.*

2 **C** is correct. This is an **inferring** question. You read *Mr Copper said he's making a display of Year Three's favourite picture books in the library for Book Week (see lines 6–8).* You can infer from this that Mr Copper is a librarian at Pablo and Inari's school. **A**, **B** and **D** are incorrect as there is no mention of Inari's father, Pablo's father or a policeman in the text.

3 **B** is correct. This is an **inferring** question. You read *It makes you laugh (see line 12)*. This implies that Inari found *The Two Bullies* an amusing picture book. **A**, **C** and **D** are incorrect as they are not thoughts that Inara describes herself having about the book.

4 **A** and **C** are correct. This is an **inferring** question. Pablo says *I'm not really that interested in red trees (see line 17)*. You can infer from this that he thinks he wouldn't like the book because he thinks it is about a subject he finds boring (**A**). You can also infer it is the title *The Red Tree* that makes him think he wouldn't like it as he isn't interested in red trees (**C**). **B** is incorrect as there is no evidence about what Pablo knows or doesn't know about red trees. **D** is incorrect because Pablo doesn't say he dislikes picture books with a lot of words.

5 **D** is correct. This is an **inferring** question. You read *Shaun Tan made that awesome movie called* The Lost Thing, *didn't he? I think I will give your red tree book a try (see lines 20–21)*. You can infer that Pablo changed his mind because he remembered he had admired a different work by the author of *The Red Tree*. This made him think that perhaps he would like *The Red Tree* as well. **A** is incorrect because Inari's summary of the story is not what made Pablo change his mind about reading it. **B** is incorrect because there is no evidence that Pablo wants to know what the surprise is in the last picture. **C** is incorrect because there is no evidence that Pablo wants to please Inari.

6 This is an **inferring** question. You can infer that both Pablo's and Inari's choices were made because of remembering how much they liked the illustrations in each of the books they chose.

Harmony Day (page 49)

1 A **2** B **3** D **4** C **5** B **6** See below

Explanations

1 **A** is correct. This is an **inferring** question. You can infer that all the activities celebrate contributions from different cultures. **B** and **D** are incorrect because it is differences between cultures and not similarity or sameness that are at the heart of the activities. **C** is incorrect because, while different places or countries are celebrated, other things such as people, activities and food from different cultures are also celebrated.

2 **B** is correct. This is an **inferring** question. You read *Wear orange: it represents Harmony Day (see box number 1)*. This means that orange would be a good choice to use in a LOGO design as it is the colour that stands for Harmony Day. **A**, **C** and **D** are incorrect as these choices are not connected with Harmony Day in any special way.

3 **D** is correct. This is an **inferring** question. The unusual thing about TheGroup's performance is that instruments from different cultures are combined. **A, B** and **C** may be true but they are not the main reason for including TheGroup in Harmony Day celebrations.

4 **C** is correct. This is an **inferring** question. The country of origin is named for each of the offerings except for the water which comes *from everywhere* (Box number 5). This is a humorous way of linking it to Harmony Day. **A, B** and **D** are incorrect as they are straightforward links between the food and its country of origin.

5 **B** is correct. This is an **inferring** question. You can infer, since you will be watching a game, that the two teams will be playing against each other. **A** is incorrect as the word victory doesn't make sense in the position it is in. **C** is incorrect because the teams would not be voting for each other when they are playing a game of football. **D** is incorrect because the teams would be doing more than viewing each other if people are watching them play a game of football.

6 This is an **inferring** question. Box number 8 describes inviting someone new to come with you and your family to the celebrations. This is the only activity that can be done before you are at the celebrations.

Why do birds fly in a V shape? (page 50)

1 A **2** C **3** C **4** D **5** See below

Explanations

1 **A** is correct. This is an **inferring** question. You read *When the birds changed positions in the V, to give the leader a rest* (see lines 16–17). This implies that there is only one leader. The illustration also shows one bird in the lead. **B, C** and **D** are incorrect because there is only one bird in the leading position.

2 **C** is correct. This is an **inferring** question. The planes are flying through the air when they fly in a V formation. You can infer that the lift the plane gets comes from movement in the air caused by the plane in front of it. **A, B** and **D** are incorrect because neither water, rain nor smoke would help lift a plane in the air.

3 **C** is correct. This is an **inferring** question. The scientists collected information about the ibises' movements in flight. You can infer that the sensors were attached to the birds to record this information. **A** is incorrect because the scientists were not sending information to the birds—they were collecting information from them. **B** is incorrect because wearing sensors (which are minute) does not make anything easier to see. **D** is incorrect because sensors do not affect the flight of the birds in any way. Their purpose is to record information about their flight.

4 **D** is correct. This is an **inferring** question. The experiment proved that the reason birds fly in a V formation is to benefit from air currents from other birds so they conserve or save their energy on long flights. **A** is incorrect because finding that flying in a V shape helps ibises keep warm is not recorded as a finding of the experiment. **B** is incorrect because it was not found that birds imitate planes, although it was confirmed that the reasons they fly in a V shape are similar. **C** is incorrect because, while it may feel comfortable for birds to fly in a V shape, this is not their reason for doing so.

5 This is an **inferring** question. You can infer that the scientists did not find out from this experiment if pelicans, storks and geese know how to save energy on long flights. It seems likely that they do but further experimenting would be needed to prove these birds behave in the same way.

How Australia got its name (page 51)

1 B **2** C **3** D **4** B **5** See below
6 See below

Explanations

1 **B** is correct. This is an **inferring** question. You read *as far back as Roman times, legends told of a land* (see line 2). *Legends* are old stories from long ago and the words *as far back as* also suggest something that took place a long time ago. **A, C** and **D** are incorrect because none of the lengths of time named are a long time ago.

2 **C** is correct. This is an **inferring** question. You read that *Terra Australia Incognita* means *'Unknown Land to the South'* (see lines 2–3).

You can infer that if there were legends about it and it was called by a name that means it was unknown, people must have been unsure if it existed. **A** is incorrect because the fact that a name sounds important is not a reason to use it to name a place you are not sure is there. **B** is incorrect because as its name suggests, the '*Unknown Land to the South*' *(see line 2)* was not well known at that time by European people. **D** is incorrect because friendliness is not how the names of countries are chosen.

3 **D** is correct. This is an **inferring** question. You can infer that Dutch explorers were from Holland and they named the 'new' land New Holland after their own country. **A** is incorrect because there is no evidence that they were tired of using a Latin name. **B** is incorrect because New South Wales was given that name after New Holland was named. **C** is incorrect. There is no evidence that the Dutch planned to shift Holland anywhere.

4 **B** is correct. This is an **inferring** question. You read *When it became a convict settlement in 1788, New South Wales named a much larger area than the present New South Wales. At that time, for example, it included parts of New Zealand* *(see lines 17–19)*. You can infer from this that New South Wales named a much larger area of land in the 1700s than it now does. **A** is incorrect because New South Wales was never home to Dutch explorers. **C** is incorrect because there were differences in the amount of territory included under the name in the late 1700s and the present. **D** is incorrect because New South Wales covered a larger area in the late 1700s, not a smaller area.

5 This is an **inferring** question. You can work out that since *Terra Australis* means *'Land of the South'* *(see lines 8–9)*, *Australis* must mean either 'land' or 'of the South'. You would not use a general word like 'land' to name a place. You can infer, then, that *Australia* means 'of the South'. [Note that this makes sense when you are looking at it from the northern hemisphere.]

6 This is an **inferring** question. New Holland and New South Wales named parts of the continent. Matthew Flinders needed a name for the whole continent to put on his map, so he chose a different name from these.

Language questions

My new puppy (page 56)

1 B **2** A **3** C **4** D **5** See below

Explanations

1 **B** is correct. This is a **language** question. Harry's puppy is a Tibetan Terrier. This is the name of the breed (type) of dog. **A** is incorrect as Harry's name for his dog is Tezza, not Tibetan Terrier. **C** is incorrect because there is no evidence that Harry's puppy was born in Tibet. **D** is incorrect as Harry's plans are for looking after a real dog, not a toy.

2 **A** is correct. This is a **language** question. The verbs that begin each step of Harry's plans (*Keep, Introduce, Persuade, Give, Give, Play*) *(see lines 6, 9, 13, 17, 19 and 20)* are in the form of commands or instructions to himself. **B**, **C** and **D** are incorrect because the verbs are not in the past tense, do not begin questions and do not make requests of Tezza.

3 **C** is correct. This is a **language** question. When Harry says *you see* *(see line 16)* he is explaining his idea about having a clock ready for Tezza in more detail to his diary. **A**, **B** and **D** are incorrect because Harry is not addressing them here. Whenever he does make a remark to Tezza, his mum or his cat, rather than to his diary, he puts it in brackets to separate it from what he is telling his diary.

4 **D** is correct. This is a **language** question. When Harry thinks about playing with Tezza he feels so excited that he repeats her name twice. **A** is incorrect because her name is easy to pronounce and Harry has had no trouble pronouncing it earlier in his diary entry. **B** is incorrect as there is no evidence that Tezza has a second name and if she did it is highly unlikely it would be Tezza. **C** is incorrect. Harry may be proud of Tezza's name and this could be part of why he repeats it. The main reason, though, is his excitement when he realises she is going to be playing games with him and be part of his life very soon.

5 This is a **language** question. Harry is having a joke with his diary by exaggerating how frightening the new puppy will be to a book made of paper that could be eaten up easily.

He adds a smiley face to show his diary he is making a joke.

In the olden days (page 57)

1 A **2** C **3** D **4** B **5** C **6** See below

Explanations

1 **A** is correct. This is a **language** question. Adding the modal word *certainly* is a way of showing you are completely sure and there is no room for doubt. **B**, **C** and **D** are incorrect because they suggest different kinds of uncertainty.

2 **C** is correct. This is a **language** question. Gran asks Molly if she is able to see the white patch. In the illustration Molly is using a magnifying glass to see it. You can work out that it is extremely small. **A** is incorrect because if something is *minute* *(see line 6)* it is not easily seen. **B** and **D** are incorrect because they name sizes that would both be easy to see.

3 **D** is correct. This is a **language** question. The exclamation mark shows that Molly is expressing feelings about what she has just been told. The word *You* is italicised to show that Molly is surprised to learn her respectable Gran was once thought disobedient. **A**, **B** and **C** are incorrect because there is no evidence that Molly feels anger, fear or sorrow about what she has been told.

4 **B** is correct. This is a **language** question. You may have heard this before and know it is an old saying. The repeated pattern of words in the sentence (*you* + *don't* + *verb*) also suggests that it could be a saying. Otherwise you can work out by a process of elimination that it must be a saying. **A** is incorrect because the sentence does not have an exclamation mark. **C** and **D** are incorrect because like things are not being compared (simile) or said to be the same as something else (metaphor).

5 **C** is correct. This is a **language** question. You read *We did have a radio and I listened to The Argonauts* *(see lines 16–17)*. The *and* in the sentence shows there is a connection between the radio and *The Argonauts*. The capital letters and italics show that *The Argonauts* is the name of something. You can work out from this that *The Argonauts* names a radio program to which Gran listened as a little girl. **B** is incorrect because Gran didn't have a TV at that time. **A** and **D** are incorrect because they have no connection with a radio.

6 This is a **language** question. The capital letters are used to show that Gran is having a joke with Molly by exaggerating what she did. It makes it seem as though she's committed a big crime and could be a danger to her granddaughter.

Country life versus city life (page 58)

1 B **2** A **3** A and C **4** D **5** See below

Explanations

1 **B** is correct. This is a **language** question. Bertie uses words with negative meanings (*pollution*, *fumes*) *(see line 3)* to persuade people that nobody would choose to breathe air that held them. **A**, **C** and **D** are incorrect as they suggest people (everybody, anybody, all) would choose to breathe air of that kind rather than sweet-smelling fresh air.

2 **A** is correct. This is a **language** question. By adding the modal word *Certainly* to his answer, Bertie is showing how definite he feels about his negative reply. **B**, **C** and **D** are incorrect because they suggest that he doesn't have strong negative feelings in answer to his question.

3 **A** and **C** are correct. This is a **language** question. Bertie's description of neighbours in the city implies that they are all *cranky* *(see line 13)*. This is an exaggeration and unlikely to be true (**A**). The adjective *screeching* makes the *sirens* sound extremely unpleasant—harsh, loud and piercing *(see line 7)*. It is true that sirens are noisy but perhaps not quite as unpleasantly so as Bertie claims. **C** is incorrect because you do hear the mooing of cows in the countryside. **D** is incorrect because it is not an exaggeration to say there is space to ride in the countryside.

4 **D** is correct. This is a **language** question. Bertie chooses these action (doing) verbs to tell about the physical actions he enjoys doing in the open spaces of the countryside. **A**, **B** and **C** are incorrect because memories, moods or thoughts name mental processes rather than physical actions.

5 This is a **language** question. Bertie means that there are no questions that could be asked that

would change his mind. He feels that there is no possible doubt about his conclusion—country life is better than city life.

City life versus country life (page 59)

1 C **2** C **3** C **4** B **5** See below

Explanations

1. C is correct. This is a **language** question. Lian makes the amount of pollution sound less than it is to give a better impression of city life. **A** and **B** are incorrect because they are the opposite of what Lian wants to do. **D** is incorrect because Lian is not trying to be accurate but to make the pollution sound unimportant.
2. C is correct. This is a **language** question. Lian's words show that she partly accepts Bertie's comment about liking the quiet of the country because she agrees it can be *nice sometimes* (see line 6). **A** and **D** are incorrect because the word *always* is opposite in meaning to *sometimes*. **B** is incorrect because Lian's comment shows that she thinks this comment of Bertie's is not a complete exaggeration.
3. C is correct. This is a **language** question. The ice-cream van plays *'Greensleeves'* (see line 7) so you can work out that it is a piece of music or a song that comes from its sound system. **A** and **B** are incorrect because you can't play a person or a place. **D** is incorrect because, while you can play a game, a van is not able to do this.
4. B is correct. This is a **language** question. *To get in someone's hair* is an idiom meaning 'irritate or pester someone'. Lian is saying that her neighbours are not like this. This means they are never a problem. **A**, **C** and **D** are incorrect as Lian is praising her neighbours so she wouldn't describe them in a negative way as useless, annoying or pests.
5. This is a **language** question. Lian says you feel *isolated* (see line 11) when you can't connect with other people. You can work out from this that *isolated* means out of touch and cut off from other people.

The whistling language (page 60)

1 C **2** B **3** B **4** D **5** See below

Explanations

1. C is correct. This is a **language** question. The whistling language is a public language used to send messages across distances in the mountains. Everyone can hear what is said when it is used. **A** is incorrect because it is not the language you use for conversations when people are nearby. **B** is incorrect because you would use it to spread the news of a baptism but you would not use it with people at the baptism. **D** is incorrect as it is not just a hobby. It is used to make serious communications with people at a distance.
2. B is correct. This is a **language** question. You read *I talked to a young Spanish boy, called Cyro, about el silbo (the whistle)* (see line 14). This suggests that the words *el silbo* are Spanish. You could also use a process of elimination to work this out as none of the other words are Spanish. **A** is incorrect because YouTube is an English word naming a video sharing service. **C** is incorrect because *canaris* (see line 23) is a Latin word. **D** is incorrect because UNESCO, as the list of capital letters suggest, stands for the name of an organisation of the United Nations.
3. B is correct. This is a **language** question. The use of capital letters means that *Down Under* (see line 20) names a particular place. People in the northern hemisphere (such as the Canary Islands) often call places in the southern hemisphere *Down Under.* Auntie Chris also uses *Oz* (see line 20), a nickname for Australia, as a synonym for *Down Under.* **A**, **C** and **D** are incorrect as these are places that would not be named with capital letters.
4. D is correct. This is a **language** question. The inclusion of the words *Perhaps* and *might* (see line 19) leave open other possibilities (known as low modality). The statement makes a suggestion without any pressure to do what it says. **A**, **B** and **C** are incorrect as they are all ways of trying to enforce that an action is done (known as high modality).
5. This is a **language** question. The words Auntie Chris uses about Australia, such as *Down Under* and *dear old Oz* (see line 20), express her feelings of affection and fondness for her home country.

Jake's jokes (page 61)

1 C **2** B **3** C **4** D **5** C **6** See below

Explanations

1 C is correct. This is a **language** question. You would try to cheer up a *blue* (see line 8) elephant because *blue* also means 'sad or depressed'. The humour in the joke relies on a pun. A pun is a play on words. You only get the joke if you recognise the pun. **A**, **B** and **D** are incorrect because if *blue* meant large (**A**), happy (**B**) or peculiar (**D**), there wouldn't be a joke.

2 **B** is correct. This is a **language** question. *Humphrey* (see line 11) is pronounced 'Humfree', which sounds similar to 'hump free', creating a pun. You only get the joke if you know how to pronounce the word *Humphrey*. **A** is incorrect because, while *Humphrey* being a camel's name is part of the humour, it is not the main part. **C** is incorrect because while the 'f' sound is difficult to spell, this is not what creates the humour. **D** is incorrect because, while *Humphrey* may be difficult to pronounce, this is not what creates the humour.

3 **C** is correct. This is a **language** question. The word *nobody* (see line 13) sounds almost the same as *no body*, which means something quite different—'without a body'. Since it is a skeleton that is being talked about, it is this second idea which makes the answer amusing. **A**, **B** and **D** are incorrect as these words are not what makes the joke amusing.

4 **D** is correct. This is a **language** question. It is the ridiculousness of the idea of birds walking south each year that makes this answer amusing. **A**, **B** and **C** are explanations that do not contain any humour.

5 **C** is correct. This is a **language** question. The words *turned into* (see line 17) have two meanings. They mean 'changed direction' and 'changed into something else'. In this case, the idea of a tractor magically turning into a field is what is humorous. **A**, **B** and **D** are incorrect because these words do not create the humour.

6 This is a **language** question. The snail's exclamation of excitement (*Wheee!!*) (see line 19) is amusing because it is so comical and unexpected. You only get the joke if you know that snails and turtles are both recognised as very slow animals on land. You realise that, for a snail, a ride on a turtle's back would be moving at a very daring speed!

Hang out@Holly's (page 62)

1 B **2** A, C, D **3** B and C **4** B
5 See below **6** See below

Explanations

1 **B** is correct. This is a **language** question. The words *hang out* (see line 14) are mainly used by young people to mean spending time together in a friendly, relaxed way. The use of the owner's first name, Holly, is another laid-back, casual touch in the name, as is using the website address format in the name. **A**, **C** and **D** are incorrect because the idea of hanging out is not an idea that suggests a formal, romantic or traditional atmosphere.

2 **A**, **C** and **D** are correct. This is a **language** question. The freshness of the food (e.g. the fresh food bar, eggs laid today, just picked fruit) and the healthy choices available (e.g. baby spinach, juices made from vegetables and fruit, etc.) are themes that are highlighted through constant references to them (**A**, **D**). The message about affordable prices, although only mentioned once, is emphasised by its prominent position in a line by itself next to the restaurant's name (**C**). **B** is incorrect because although directions to get to the restaurant are provided, they are on a link to a map that is tucked away at the bottom of the web page and not emphasised.

3 **B** and **C** are correct. This is a **language** question. *Newly baked* (see line 10) is an accurate, factual description of when the bread was baked, as is *homemade* (see line 18) of how the ice-cream was made. **A** is incorrect as fruit does not actually burst with goodness or sunshine. **D** is incorrect because juices may be thought of as *dreamy* (see line 12) but they are not really made of dreams.

4 **B** is correct. This is a **language** question. The words *(laid today!)* (see line 10) are put in brackets to emphasise that all the hard-boiled eggs served in the restaurant are freshly laid on the day of serving. **A** and **D**

are incorrect because the statement is not about the kind of eggs chickens lay but about when the restaurant uses the freshly laid eggs. **C** is incorrect because this statement means that the restaurant could boil the eggs daily without them being newly laid eggs.

5 This is a **language** question. Evidence that shows this is a website advertisement include:
   - internet language, such as @ and the web address, www.hangout@holly's.com.qld.au (see line 2)
   - clickable words, such as *Read more* and *Click here for a map* (see lines 29 and 32) that require the reader to go to another screen to find the extra information.

Dot and the Kangaroo (page 63)

1 B **2** A **3** C **4** B **5** D **6** See below

Explanations

1 **B** is correct. This is a **language** question. The Kangaroo is a particular kangaroo in the story. She has a character and personality of her own. Giving her a capital letter is like naming her for the story. **A** is unlikely because most authors know when to use capital letters. (You might have noticed that the author gives the word Human a capital letter to show the Kangaroo thinks of humans in a special way, so this shows she makes careful choices.) **C** is incorrect as this is a made-up grammar rule that no-one follows. **D** is incorrect. The Kangaroo may be important in her mob, but this is not the reason the word is given a capital letter in the story.

2 **A** is correct. This is a **language** question. The idiom *jump to conclusions* (see line 6) means guessing an answer without waiting to know all the facts. When the Kangaroo says it, she gives it a literal meaning which is comical. She means she literally jumps about a lot rather than thinking. **B** is incorrect because the sentence is not making a comparison. **C** is incorrect because not everything the Kangaroo says is comical. There are many animal stories where animals speak without creating humour. **D** is incorrect because the Kangaroo is seriously concerned about Dot and trying to help her not get a headache; her behaviour is not meant to be clown-like.

3 **C** is correct. This is a **language** question. When the Kangaroo uses the word *everyone* (see line 11) she includes Dot along with the kangaroos. She thinks because kangaroos get thirsty at sundown, so does Dot. **A** is incorrect as it doesn't tell you anything about what the Kangaroo thinks. **B** and **D** are incorrect because they are things said by Dot so they don't tell the reader anything about what the Kangaroo thinks.

4 **B** is correct. This is a **language** question. The Kangaroo feels sorry for the *Poor little Human* (see line 15) who is thirsty, tired and weak. This makes her look sympathetically at Dot and offer her a ride in her pouch to the water-hole. **A** is incorrect as it is the opposite of the way the Kangaroo looks at Dot. **C** and **D** are incorrect because they are not feelings that would lead the Kangaroo to say *Poor little Human*.

5 **D** is correct. This is a **language** question. The reader sees that Dot took the Kangaroo's advice and stepped *Timidly and carefully* into her pouch — *the cosiest, softest little bag imaginable* (see lines 17–18). This means that Dot did what the Kangaroo told her to do. **A** is incorrect because Dot did what the Kangaroo asked; she did not turn away. **B** is incorrect as there is no evidence that Dot asked the Kangaroo for help at this moment. **C** is incorrect because Dot did the opposite of this; she followed the Kangaroo's advice.

6 This is a **language** question. The Kangaroo is exaggerating how quickly they will get there in order to reassure Dot about their journey. It doesn't take any time at all for a locust to shrill so if they take even less time than this to get to the water-hole, it will be a very quick journey.

Judgement questions

Matilda (page 68)

1 B **2** A **3** D **4** D **5** See below

Explanations

1 **B** is correct. This is a **judgement** question. You judge that the house is grand because it has a ballroom, more than one floor and many

pictures. **A**, **C** and **D** are incorrect because they are homes that do not have these features.

2 **A** is correct. This is a **judgement** question. You judge that Matilda's actions put her own and others' lives in danger. This is confirmed when Matilda's actions lead to her death. **B**, **C** and **D** are incorrect because they suggest that Matilda's actions are harmless rather than dangerous.

3 **D** is correct. This is a **judgement** question. The rhymes emphasise its humour by making fun of, or mocking, the seriousness of what is being said (e.g. *Matilda / very nearly killed her*) *(see lines 6–7)*. **A** is incorrect because the seriousness of the tale lies in its moral and not in telling it in rhyme. **B** is incorrect because although the end is sad in that Matilda is burned to death, the poem is told in a comical way. **C** is incorrect because no-one acts bitterly in the tale.

4 **D** is correct. This is a **judgement** question. You judge that Matilda's Aunt is not bad tempered because, even after Matilda calls the Fire Brigade, her Aunt does her best to sort things out without losing her temper. **A** is incorrect as it takes Matilda's Aunt a very long time to stop believing what Matilda tells her, even though Matilda lies all the time. **B** is incorrect as Matilda's Aunt owns a big house in London and has enough money to pay the Fire Brigade for their trouble. **C** is incorrect as Matilda's Aunt is truthful and tries to do the right thing.

5 This is a **judgement** question. The moral is not to tell lies as it is always wrong to do so. The tale makes it clear that telling lies can lead to people no longer believing anything you say. It can even lead to disaster.

Blogging about bags (page 69)

1 C **2** B **3** A **4** D **5** A **6** See below

Explanations

1 **C** is correct. This is a **judgement** question. You judge that Belinda's attitude changes because she finds out things about plastic bags that show they are not harmless. **A** is incorrect because the opposite is true—she learns not to appreciate them. **B** is incorrect because there is no evidence that Belinda is always changing her mind. **D** is incorrect as her blog entry about plastic bags is made after she changes her mind about them.

2 **B** is correct. This is a **judgement** question. You judge that it is impossible for researchers to know the exact number of animals whose death is caused, so they work out a rough figure or estimate. **A** is incorrect because it is not Belinda who does the counting. **C** is incorrect because *estimated* *(see line 4)* is not strictly a scientific term and there is no evidence that Belinda is showing off. **D** is incorrect because the researchers have a rough idea of how many animals die as a result of swallowing or getting tangled in plastic bags.

3 **A** is correct. This is a **judgement** question. You judge that a situation which causes the death of so many animals is a *shocking truth* *(see line 4)*. **B**, **C** and **D** are incorrect because to describe the situation as *shocking* is not to exaggerate or to be careless or inaccurate. It is *shocking* to learn that the deaths of vast numbers of animals are caused by plastic bags.

4 **D** is correct. This is a **judgement** question. You judge that Belinda's family's response is supportive because together they decide to take action against using plastic bags. **A** and **B** are incorrect because the family's actions are the opposite of unenthusiastic and disapproving. **C** is incorrect because there is no evidence that the family is bored.

5 **A** is correct. This is a **judgement** question. Plastic bags not biodegrading means they pollute the soil and the ocean with their poisons. You judge that this makes the situation even more serious. **B** and **D** are incorrect because they are the opposite of the truth of the situation. **C** is incorrect because it makes the situation of great concern, rather than of no concern.

6 This is a **judgement** question. You judge that people often don't manage to stick to their plans even though they mean to do so. However, Belinda and her family sound very concerned and upset about the problem, so it seems quite likely they will manage to stick to their plan.

Fire at magic shop (page 70)

1 C **2** A **3** C **4** A **5** See below

Explanations

1 **C** is correct. This is a **judgement** question. The names of people (*Mrs Spell*, *Mr Black* and *Mr Quench*) (see lines 11, 16 and 19) are all so closely linked to their jobs that you judge it cannot be a coincidence. This suggests that their names are not believable and are part of the humour of the article. **A** and **B** are incorrect because the names make the article less believable and serious, not more so. **D** is incorrect because there is no confusion caused by the names. It is clear that they are invented for the purposes of the article.

2 **A** is correct. This is a **judgement** question. You judge that the address uses words related to magic—tricks and conjuring. This alerts the reader to the idea that it is a fake address and that the report is not serious. **B**, **C** and **D** are incorrect because the address is a joke so could not be used to locate the shop.

3 **C** is correct. This is a **judgement** question. You judge that Mrs Spell is bewildered because she can't understand how the fire began when no-one was there. **A**, **B** and **D** are incorrect because Mrs Spell shows no signs of being satisfied, amused or pleased about what has happened.

4 **A** is correct. This is a **judgement** question. You judge that Mr Black is suspicious because he thinks events have not followed a normal pattern. **B**, **C** and **D** are incorrect because Mr Black shows no signs of being horrified, disappointed or sad.

5 This is a **judgement** question. The news article pretends to be a serious article but it makes fun of, or sends up, the idea of a magic shop having magical powers.

The Swagman (page 71)

1 B **2** C **3** D **4** C **5** See below

Explanations

1 **B** is correct. This is a **judgement** question. You read *I sometimes think: When I'm a man* (see line 26). You judge that the narrator is the young boy in the poem who tells about his meeting with a swagman. **A**, **C** and **D** are incorrect because the swagman in the poem is an elderly man who speaks to the boy but does not tell the story of the poem.

2 **C** is correct. This is a **judgement** question. You read *His billy-can, as black as black, / Was just the thing for making tea / At picnics, so it seemed to me* (see lines 9–11). The boy admires everything about the swagman's billy-can. He talks about it being perfect for a picnic, which is a happy occasion. **A** and **D** are incorrect because there is no evidence that the boy dislikes or resents the billy-can. **B** is incorrect because the boy isn't offered the billy-can so he can't be grateful for it.

3 **D** is correct. This is a **judgement** question. The swagman's words warn the young boy that being on the road when you are old is very hard work. He tells the boy to avoid it if he can. This suggests he is regretful that his life has led him to the state he is now in. **A**, **B** and **C** are incorrect as they describe feelings that are the opposite of how the swagman feels, looking back.

4 **C** is correct. This is a **judgement** question. You read *and when / I laughed he made them dance again* (see lines 16–17). You judge it was the boy's laughter that led the swagman to make the corks on his hat bob about a second time. **A** is incorrect because, although the corks were there to keep the flies away, you judge he deliberately made them bob to please the boy. **B** is incorrect because he didn't do this out of habit, but rather on purpose. **D** is incorrect because although the first time they bobbed may have been caused by his head shaking sadly, the second time definitely isn't.

5 This is a **judgement** question. The boy sees the life of the swagman as filled with pleasures, such as having a billy-can to make your tea out in the open air and wearing a hat with bobbing corks. He doesn't understand the swagman's warning that it is not a good life when you are an old man.

An advertisement from 1900 (page 72)

1 B **2** A **3** B **4** A and C **5** See below

Explanations

1 **B** is correct. This is a **judgement** question. The picture sends the message that something special is needed to wash the dirty marks from the child. It also provides the answer—a cake of Pears soap (the brand name printed on it) which is beside the water, waiting to be

used. The word *Pears* in large print confirms that this is the product being advertised. **A** is incorrect as it is Pears soap, and not the fruit, that is being advertised. **C** and **D** are incorrect as there is no evidence that either the dog or the shoes are for sale.

2 **A** is correct. This is a **judgement** question. You judge that the picture shows the child lives in a comfortable home and is happy and well looked after. The child is dirty from playing with the coal but the advertisement suggests that this problem will be solved by a caring adult using Pears soap to successfully wash the dirt away. **B** is incorrect as the child, although grubby, looks happy rather than sad. **C** is incorrect. There are no signs of household poverty shown in the advertisement. **D** is incorrect. The child is dirty but does not look neglected.

3 **B** is correct. This is a **judgement** question. The advertisers choose a comfortable, well-furnished setting to associate Pears soap with families who are well off and look after their children properly. **A**, **C** and **D** are incorrect because the advertisement is not about rough dogs, naughty children or stray animals.

4 **A** and **C** are correct. This is a **judgement** question. You judge that modern children usually don't wear clothes with lace and layers of ruffles (**A**). When they get dirty they have a bath or shower rather than washing in an old-fashioned china basin with a pattern of flowers and leaves (**C**). **B** and **D** are incorrect because in advertisements of any time period a dog might have a bow and a room might be comfortable and cosy

5 This is a **judgement** question. You judge that the advertisement is aimed mainly at mothers. They are the people most likely to choose the kind of soap used in a household in the early 1900s.

The perils of palm oil (page 73)

1 A **2** A, C, D **3** C **4** B **5** See below

Explanations

1 **A** is correct. This is a **judgement** question. You read *By 2020 the demand for palm oil is expected to double* (see lines 26–27). You judge that as the world population grows, there will be an increased demand for palm oil to make the products people want. **B** is incorrect because more, not less, palm oil will be needed to meet future demands. **C** is incorrect because the demand for palm oil will not remain the same with a growing population. **D** is incorrect as there is no evidence that the demand for palm oil will disappear.

2 **A**, **C** and **D** are correct. This is a **judgement** question. The image is included to catch attention, to arouse feelings of sympathy and pity for homeless orang-utans, and to inform people of the connection between cutting down forests for palm-oil production and orang-utans being threatened with extinction. **B** is incorrect because showing people what an orang-utan looks like is not the purpose of including its image on the website.

3 **C** is correct. This is a **judgement** question. News about a new chain of supermarkets is not relevant to this website. **A** is incorrect because the website is concerned with labelling systems for palm-oil products. **B** is incorrect because endangered animals are a concern of the website. **D** is incorrect because you judge that deforestation could have an impact on climate change.

4 **B** is correct. This is a **judgement** question. The name of the respected organisation, the World Wildlife Fund, makes the information on the website seem more reliable and believable. **A** is incorrect as using highly exaggerated language would make the information less believable. **C** is incorrect because you cannot judge how believable information is from the amount that is included. **D** is incorrect because a picture of an orang-utan does not make the information on the website more believable.

5 This is a **judgement** question. Suggestions might include how you could:
- learn more about what is really happening
- use your voice to tell others about this crisis
- protest against endangering the lives of animals
- avoid buying packaged products that contain palm-tree oil not made in a sustainable way.

Natural wonders (page 74)

1 B **2** D **3** A **4** C **5** See below

Explanations

1. **B** is correct. This is a **judgement** question. You judge that these are part of nature and not created by humans. **A** is incorrect because, while it is true that these wonders are unusual, this is not what makes them *natural* (see line 2). **C** is incorrect because these places are not natural because of the money earned by their owners from tourism. **D** is incorrect because, while it is true that their environments need special care, this is not what makes them natural.
2. **D** is correct. This is a **judgement** question. You judge that Uluru is a sacred site but the other two places are not. (The name, *The Twelve Apostles*, does have reference to the Bible but it is not treated as a sacred site.) (see line 13). **A** is incorrect because all three places are located in Australia. **B** is incorrect because you judge that all three would be tourist attractions. **C** is incorrect because they have all existed for millions of years.
3. **A** is correct. This is a **judgement** question. The author's concerned attitude to environmental matters shows in the many comments about this matter and the kind of detail included. **B** and **D** are incorrect because the information is reported in a responsible, concerned way rather than a highly anxious or despairing way. **C** is incorrect because there is no evidence of a lack of concern.
4. **C** is correct. This is a **judgement** question. Each of the natural wonders has existed for more than ten million years. This has contributed to their fame. **A** is incorrect because none of the natural wonders is manmade. **B** and **D** are incorrect. There is no evidence in the text that Uluru is under serious environmental threat (**B**) or that Uluru is owned by the government (**D**).
5. This is a **judgement** question. You judge that the information about Australia's wonders is presented factually rather than in a persuasive way to attract tourists. This makes it unlikely that it would be a suitable style for an advertisement.

Clancy of the Overflow (page 75)

1 D **2** B **3** C **4** C **5** See below

Explanations

1. **D** is correct. This is a **judgement** question. The narrator says he addressed the letter *for want of better / Knowledge* (see lines 2–4). You judge that he didn't know the full address or whether Clancy was still at that address. He put his name hoping (*just 'on spec'*) (see line 8) that it would find him. **A** is incorrect because the narrator is not confident that putting Clancy's name on the letter will be enough to find him. **B** is incorrect because the address is incomplete but not because he thought the postman wouldn't need a full address. He would have put the full address if he'd known it. **C** is incorrect because Clancy didn't know the address so he couldn't have remembered it.
2. **B** is correct. This is a **judgement** question. You read *And an answer came directed in a writing unexpected* (see lines 10–11). It was the writing that was unexpected. You judge that this was because it wasn't Clancy's writing but that of a mate of his. **A** is incorrect because, although it was surprising to see it was written in tar, this is not what the narrator says he finds unexpected. **C** is incorrect because there is no delay in the reply—the answer came straight back. **D** is incorrect because the news it brought was not good in the narrator's eyes, as he was hoping to contact Clancy.
3. **C** is correct. This is a **judgement** question. You judge that the narrator sees Clancy as someone with a big reputation. He looks up to him and thinks his way of life is admirable. **A** and **B** are incorrect because there is no mention of Clancy being humble or rowdy. **D** is incorrect because he admires Clancy and his lifestyle but doesn't claim he is his best friend.
4. **C** is correct. This is a **judgement** question. You judge that the narrator knows nothing about Clancy's life as a drover. What he does say about it comes from his imagination—his *fancy visions* (see line 18) as he calls them. When he knew Clancy he was a shearer. **A** is incorrect because the narrator does not know where Clancy goes droving (other than possibly in Queensland if the letter had reliable information). **B** is incorrect because the narrator only imagines Clancy sings while droving. He doesn't know for a fact that he does. **D** is incorrect because the narrator imagines droving is full of pleasures but

he doesn't know if that is how Clancy feels about it.

5 This is a **judgement** question. The narrator imagines life in the bush is happy, relaxed and carefree. He envies a life where you have time to watch the seasons come and go. In contrast, his life in the city is filled with deadlines and demands that never seem to stop.

Mixed questions

Bees (page 76)

1 D **2** C **3** D **4** B **5** See below

Explanations

1 **D** is correct. This is a **fact-finding** question. The answer is stated directly in the text. You read *Like all insects their bodies have three parts (see line 2)*. It is a characteristic of being an insect to have a body with three parts. **A** is incorrect because the number of eyes something has does not indicate it is an insect. **B** is incorrect because hair on the body is not a sign of being an insect. **C** is incorrect because being able to sting is not confined to insects.

2 **C** is correct. This is an **inferring** question. You read *The hair that covers parts of a bee's body, including its eyes, collects pollen (see lines 4–5)*. You can infer that it is unusual for any creature to have hairs growing from its eyes. **A** and **B** are incorrect because they are both untrue statements rather than unusual facts. The bees' legs store the pollen, not the eyes (**A**). The bees' eyes do not have a sense of smell (**B**). **D** is incorrect because there is no evidence in the text to say that bees use their eyes to see in the dark.

3 **D** is correct. This is a **judgement** question. You judge that the beehive is like a society where each member has a role to play and work to do. **A** is incorrect because the queen bee has a vital role in the hive and is very important. **B** is incorrect because it is the workers who do most of the work, not the drones. **C** is incorrect because, although the bees have sent information to other bees through their waggling dance, there is no evidence that they enjoy dancing together.

4 **B** is correct. This is a **judgement** question. You read *For bees to fill their stomachs with nectar, they have to visit about 2000 flowers (see lines 14–15)*. You judge that this would take a long, rather than a short, time. **A** is incorrect because it is true that there are many different species of bee. **C** is incorrect because you judge, since precious nectar and the queen's eggs are stored there, that this must be a safe storage place. **D** is incorrect because some bees die from exhaustion caused by overwork.

5 This is an **inferring** question. The bees live in a society where they depend on each other so they must have ways of communicating. An example is the waggling dance the scout bees perform to pass on information about where to find nectar.

Fact file: bees (page 77)

1 C **2** A and D **3** C **4** B **5** See below

Explanations

1 **C** is correct. This is a **synthesis** question. The information is organised in dot points, listing facts about bees. **A** is incorrect because the points are not in the form of stories. **B** and **D** are incorrect because the information is arranged as a series of facts, not as arguments or ideas.

2 **A** and **D** are correct. This is a **fact-finding** question. The answer is stated directly in the text. You read *When a bee stings it dies soon afterwards. The stings can be fatal for people with allergies (see line 10)*. **B** is incorrect because the bee dies after the first sting so it cannot sting again. **C** is incorrect because a bee sting does not necessarily lead to an infection.

3 **C** is correct. This is a **fact-finding** question. The answer is stated directly in the text. You read *Many species of bees are solitary and don't live in hives (see line 8)*. This means that many bees live alone so it is untrue that all bees live in hives. **A**, **B** and **D** are incorrect as it is true that males have no sting, pharaohs used the bee as a symbol of royalty and loss of habitat is a threat to bees.

4 **B** is correct. This is a **fact-finding** question. The answer is stated directly in the text. You read *Pollination ... allows fertilisation so that seeds can be produced and new plants grow (see lines 12–13)*. (The collected pollen on bees' bodies touches flowers and plants so

pollination occurs automatically.) **A** and **C** are incorrect because pollination does not cause the death of bees or of plants. **D** is incorrect because bees are not made angry when they pollinate plants.

5 This is a **judgement** question. You judge that bees have an important role in food production. If whole colonies are disappearing and people don't know how to prevent this, bees may become endangered and food supplies will be threatened.

Just in Time (Part 1) (page 78)

1 C **2** B **3** A and C **4** B **5** See below

Explanations

1 **C** is correct. This is a **language** question. *Creep* means 'move slowly and carefully'. You read *His parents told him to stay away from them* [the kittens] *(see line 3)*. Tom *creeps* through the hole, hoping his parents won't hear or see him going to see the kittens. **A** is incorrect because *creep* implies that Tom went quietly and slowly. It doesn't suggest that he made himself smaller to fit into a space. **B** is incorrect because there is no evidence that he is playing a game with anyone. **D** is incorrect because there is no evidence that he wanted to frighten the kittens.

2 **B** is correct. This is a **fact-finding** question. The answer is stated directly in the text. You read *Billy liked to rub his nose against Tom's leg (see line 6)*. **A**, **C** and **D** are incorrect because, while Billy may have liked doing these things, we are not directly told that he did like any of them.

3 **A** and **C** are correct. This is a **judgement** question. You judge that most modern classrooms use whiteboards and pens rather than chalk and a blackboard. Desks don't usually have holes for inkwells because students don't write with pens dipped in ink. Desks with inkwell holes have mostly disappeared from classrooms. **B** is incorrect because children could run towards the window in an old-fashioned or a modern classroom setting. **D** is incorrect. You read *The class was silent for once, working at Maths (see lines 12–13)*. A class could work silently at Maths in either an old-fashioned or a modern classroom setting.

4 **B** is correct. This is an **inferring** question. You read that Billy *had a very loud purr! (see lines 6–7)*. When Mr Brown hears a vibratory noise nearby you can work out that it is Billy's purring that he can hear. **A** and **C** are incorrect because those sounds do not come from nearby. **D** is incorrect because there is no evidence that Tom breathes loudly. In fact we are told that *Tom hardly dared to breathe (see line 18)*.

5 This is a **judgement** question. Tom thinks Billy has given himself away with his loud purring and Mr Brown is coming towards him to find out what he has in his desk. You can judge that Tom feels nervous and scared that he is about to be found out and get into big trouble.

Just in Time (Part 2) (page 79)

1 B **2** D **3** D **4** A **5** B **6** See below

Explanations

1 **B** is correct. This is an **inferring** question. A *dais* is a low platform. You can work that out because Mr Brown *stepped down from his dais (see line 3)*. **A** is incorrect because it suggests that the dais isn't something that is high off the ground, such as a desk or chair (**D**). **C** is incorrect as you also know that Mr Brown is a teacher and not a King, so he wouldn't have a throne to step down from.

2 **D** is correct. This is a **fact-finding** question. The answer is stated directly in the text. You read *Billy thought this was a new game and pushed his tail up through the hole again! (see lines 8–9)*. **A** is incorrect because it is untrue. **B** is incorrect because there is no evidence that Billy thought this. **C** is incorrect because needing space was not the reason that he put his tail through the hole again. He was playing a game.

3 **D** is correct. This is a **synthesis** question. Billy had waved his tail before any of the other things happened. It was Billy's waving tail (**D**) that lead Mr Brown to ask Tom what was waving about on his desk (**A**). Tom had his brainwave (**C**) which allowed him to get Billy out of the desk and under his jumper.

4 **A** is correct. This is an **inferring** question. You can infer that Tom dropped his pencils to distract Mr Brown so he'd have time

to get Billy out of his desk. **B** is incorrect because there is no evidence that Tom was showing off. **C** is incorrect as there was not time to teach Billy anything. **D** is incorrect because confusing Billy would have been no help to Tom.

5 **B** is correct. This is a **judgement** question. You judge that Mr Brown is firm because he won't let Tom keep the kitten in the classroom. He also acts in a kind-hearted and understanding way by not embarrassing Tom in front of the other children. **A** is incorrect because, on the whole, Mr Brown acts wisely and not in a foolish or silly way. **C** is incorrect. Mr Brown is quite strict but he is not mean because he is gentle with Tom. **D** is incorrect as there is no evidence of Mr Brown behaving in a crabby or unpleasant way.

6 This is a **synthesis** question. The title you choose should be what the story is mainly about. You could name it, for example, *Tom and the kitten*, *Tom's brainwave* or *Tom's lucky escape*.

First Nations Australian trackers (page 80)

1 C **2** C **3** A **4** B **5** See below

Explanations

1 **C** is correct. This is an **inferring** question. You read *When they look closely at size, depth and spacing of tracks they can tell how quickly a person or animal is moving, its gender, and where it is heading* (see lines 5–7). This shows that First Nations Australian trackers understand the meaning of the signs they see in their surroundings. **A** and **B** are partly how First Nations trackers 'read' the land, but it is their skill in understanding the meanings of what they see and hear that is important. **D** is incorrect as reading the land is different from telling stories about the land.

2 **C** is correct. This is a **fact-finding** question. The answer is stated directly in the text. You read *Sometimes they spend hours in one spot scanning the ground for signs of the beginning of a track* (see lines 3–5). **A** is incorrect because, although the trackers work out where a track is heading, they do this after they find where it begins. **B** is incorrect because, although the trackers look closely at the size of tracks, they do this after they find where it begins. **D** is incorrect because First Nations trackers do not use magic—they use their knowledge and skills.

3 **A** is correct. This is an **inferring** question. It was amazing that the First Nations trackers were able to find the children so quickly. The locals had searched for over a week for the lost children but had failed to find them. **B** is incorrect. While it is true that one of the trackers was an Australian cricketer, this is not what made their finding the children amazing. **C** is incorrect as there is no evidence in the text that the First Nations trackers were surprised to find the children. **D** is incorrect because it is not clear from what is said whether they were found together or separately.

4 **B** is correct. This is a **fact-finding** question. The answer is stated directly in the text. You read *First Nations Australian trackers have helped locate criminals and bushrangers. A famous example of this is when they helped police capture Ned Kelly* (see lines 20–23). **A** and **D** are incorrect as major Mitchell and Edward John Eyre are explorers, not bushrangers. **C** is incorrect as Glenrowan is the name of a town, not of a bushranger.

5 This is a **judgement** question. You judge that First Nations trackers are famous for using their knowledge and skills to help people and save lives. They have helped explorers survive, found people who are lost and helped police locate dangerous criminals.

I remember (page 81)

1 C **2** A **3** B **4** C **5** B **6** See below

Explanations

1 **C** is correct. This is an **inferring** question. Bindy uses large letters to reinforce the idea of how large the playground looked to her. **A** is incorrect because there is no evidence in the text that she likes the look of capital letters. **B** is incorrect because she could have corrected her mistake if she'd wanted to. **D** is incorrect because there is no evidence in the text that Bindy is trying to attract attention.

2 **A** is correct. This is an **inferring** question. You read *I followed the teacher everywhere* (see lines 5–6). The teacher says Bindy is like a duckling because she follows her as if she is

the mother duck and Bindy a duckling. **B** is incorrect because the teacher smiles in a kind, rather than an unkind, way when she says this. **C** and **D** are incorrect because there is no evidence in the text that the teacher loves Bindy or ducklings, or that she wants to make Bindy get out of her way.

3 **B** is correct. This is a **fact-finding** question. The answer is stated directly in the text. When everyone crowds around her, Bindy feels as if she's famous. **A**, **C** and **D** are incorrect as these are not the things that make Bindy feel famous.

4 **C** is correct. This is a **fact-finding** question. The answer is stated directly in the text. Bindy wears her watch in the bath. It stops working because it is not waterproof. **A** is incorrect because if the watch were waterproof it would not stop working when put under the water. **B** and **D** are incorrect as there is no evidence that Bindy's watch is faulty or that it loses time.

5 **B** is correct. This is an **inferring** question. You read *I pretended I was an ambulance and went really fast* (see line 18). An ambulance travels quickly to get to people who need help. This implies that Bindy went quickly on her scooter because she was pretending to be an ambulance. **A** is incorrect because, although she may have loved going fast, the reason she did so was because she was pretending to be an ambulance. **C** and **D** are incorrect as there is no evidence that she was testing her scooter's speed limit or that she was showing her friends how quickly she could go.

6 This is a **synthesis** question. Bindy's memories of when she was younger are most often about things going wrong for her, such as having an accident or getting sick. Even her happiest memory is about pretending to be an ambulance!

Colours and their meanings (page 82)

1 B **2** A **3** C **4** B **5** B, C and D
6 See below

Explanations

1 **B** is correct. This is a **fact-finding** question. The answer is stated directly in the text. You read *You 'see red' when you are angry* (see line 3). **A**, **C** and **D** are incorrect because red does not stand for love, the heart or romance in this idiom.

2 **A** is correct. This is a **language** question. The phrase *on the other hand* (see lines 3–4) introduces the information that the colour red can have an opposite connection in people's minds. The phrase suggests an exception will follow, as does the word *however*. **B**, **C** and **D** are incorrect as it is not information of the same kind that is being added. These answers all imply something more rather than something different.

3 **C** is correct. This is a **language** question. The word *national* (see line 5) means 'of the nation or country'. This suggests that national colours will arouse people's feelings of connection with their country. Answers **A**, **B** and **D** are incorrect as national colours are not connected with personal sporting teams, colour choices or schools so they will not arouse people's feelings of connection with these.

4 **B** is correct. This is an **inferring** question. You can work out that suffering from jealousy is a kind of sickness that makes you look greenish. **A**, **C** and **D** are incorrect as they don't explain the comparison that is being made.

5 **B**, **C** and **D** are correct. This is a **synthesis** question. The meanings a colour stands for do sometimes change over time (**B**). Some countries think differently about what particular colours symbolise. (**C**). Idioms or symbols are examples of how colours can be used to communicate meanings (**D**). **A** is incorrect because there is evidence in the text that colours have fixed meanings.

6 This is a **judgment** question. Answers will vary. Your answer can't be right or wrong. It will depend on your personal choice and the connections your choice of colour has for you.

The Indigenous Round (page 83)

1 B **2** B **3** B **4** A **5** See below

Explanations

1 **B** is correct. This is a **language** question. You can work out that a round has more than one match because it involves a series of games between two sides. **A** is incorrect because, although a round is a circle, it is not the meaning of a round in this phrase. **C** is

incorrect because the round happens each year so it is not a game that is completed. **D** is incorrect because, although a round can be a song, it is not what is meant in this phrase about football matches.

2 **B** is correct. This is an **inferring** question. You can work out that the Hawks is a team made up of First Nations and non-Indigenous people who play games of football together. **A**, **C** and **D** are incorrect because both First Nations and non-Indigenous players are part of the Hawks.

3 **B** is correct. This is a **judgement** question. You judge that the positive way the First Nations Round is described suggests the author is in its favour and approves of what it celebrates. **A**, **C** and **D** are incorrect because there is no evidence that the author disapproves, is concerned or lacks interest in the idea of an Indigenous Round.

4 **A** is correct. This is a **language** question. You read that a curtain-raiser is part of the entertainment that takes place before the match. You can work out that it is an event that warms up the audience or serves to raise the curtain (not a real curtain, of course) for the main event. **B** is incorrect because the curtain-raiser described here has the purpose of showing the talents of First Nations footballers from around Australia. **C** is incorrect because this suggests it comes after rather than before the main event. **D** is incorrect because the curtain-raiser has its own importance in the celebration.

5 This is a **synthesis** question. Wearing Indigenous jerseys is a way that all players show respect for First Nations peoples, their culture and heritage. It is also a way of acknowledging the traditional owners of the land where the football games are played.

Should weekend sport be compulsory? (page 84)

1 B **2** C **3** B **4** B **5** D **6** See below

Explanations

1 **B** is correct. This is a **fact-finding** question. The answer is stated directly in the text. Tchi says *You need to make the choice for yourself though* (see lines 10–11). This means Tchi thinks the choice should be your own and that you should not be made to play sport. **A**, **C** and **D** are incorrect because none of the other students says this, although Jem does think it is a sensible idea even though he feels it would not work for him.

2 **C** is correct. This is a **synthesis** question. The main reason Liz thinks boys and girls need compulsory weekend sport is because she thinks they spend too much time with technology and not enough time exercising. **A** is incorrect because, although Liz thinks her brothers don't exercise enough, this is only part of her reason. **B** is incorrect because it is not what she argues. **D** is incorrect because Liz may think this but she does not use the idea to support her point of view.

3 **B** is correct. This is a **language** question. Jem is saying Tchi's idea is *sensible* (see line 17), but that he himself is not sensible. He is making a joke against himself. **A** is incorrect because Jem is disagreeing, rather than agreeing, with Tchi's point of view when he says this. **C** is incorrect because Jem is disagreeing with Tchi, not Liz. **D** is incorrect because Jem does not mention cricket when he says this.

4 **B** is correct. This is an **inferring** question. Amy says *it could be compulsory for girls but definitely not for boys* (see lines 22–24). This opinion is based on whether a person is male or female. You can infer that this is why Jem says *That's sexist, Amy. Why not boys?* (see line 25). **A**, **C** and **D** are incorrect because Amy doesn't comment on a person's attitude, character or behaviour when she makes the comment that Jem thinks is sexist.

5 **D** is correct. This is a **synthesis** question. Tchi disagrees with Liz and Jem, who both support compulsory weekend sport. Amy thinks boys should not have to do compulsory weekend sport. This means that the two who voted against it would be Tchi and Amy. **A**, **B** and **C** are incorrect because they give the wrong combination of names.

6 This is a **judgement** question. Answers will vary. Your answer will depend on your own attitude to the question and whether you find the arguments put forward by any of the students convincing and well reasoned.

When I grow up (page 85)

1 D **2** B **3** B **4** A **5** A **6** See below

Explanations

1 **D** is correct. This is a **fact-finding** question The answer is stated directly in the text. In the first verse, the narrator says *When I grow up / I plan to be / someone who lives / by the sea* *(see lines 2–5)*. **A**, **B** and **C** name plans mentioned in later verses.

2 **B** is correct. This is a **language** question. The narrator thinks of flying a plane as a way to earn money to stay out of debt. **A** is incorrect because too much money is the opposite of having a debt. **C** and **D** are incorrect because while being in *debt* *(see line 11)* might get you into trouble or even prison, prison is not what the word means.

3 **B** is correct. This is a **judgement** question. The mother recognises that all her child's plans are just dreams, which makes her attitude realistic. **A**, **C** and **D** are incorrect because there is no evidence of her being disappointed, anxious or over excited.

4 **A** is correct. This is a **judgement** question. The mood is set by the child who has a positive, happy attitude to growing up and to all the possibilities that lie ahead. **B**, **C** and **D** are incorrect as there is no evidence of these moods in the poem.

5 **A** is correct. This is an **inferring** question. You can infer that most of the activities described involve doing things in an active, physical way—swimming, sailing, surfing, and so on. **B**, **C** and **D** are incorrect because only a few of the narrator's dreams involve bravery, usefulness or difficulty.

6 This is a **judgement** question. The narrator is an easygoing, friendly sounding person. You judge that he or she accepts Mum's criticism without becoming cross or annoyed, and acknowledges she was *quite right* when she said '*You're dreaming*' *(see line 26)*. At the same time the narrator has an optimistic attitude towards the future and thinks many interesting possibilities lie ahead.

Henry Lawson's bush school (page 86)

1 B **2** A **3** D **4** B **5** B **6** See below

Explanations

1 **B** is correct. This is a **fact-finding** question. The answer is stated directly in the text. You read *His father … built the school out of bark* *(see lines 4–5)*. **A**, **C** and **D** are incorrect as they name people and an organisation that did not build the old bush school.

2 **A** is correct. This is an **inferring** question. You can work out that coming from Ireland, John Tiernan was not used to the Australian bush. He was afraid that the bark, from which the school was made, would not stand up to storms. **B** is incorrect as having his home attached is not a reason for the school to fall down. **C** is incorrect because the number of children is not relevant to whether the school would fall down in a storm. **D** is incorrect because there is no evidence that he believed Irish schools often fell down.

3 **D** is correct. This is a **language** question. The inverted commas are used as quotation marks. The words in the quotation marks are things Henry has said about his school. **A** is incorrect because the words the inverted commas are put around are not old-fashioned words. **B** is incorrect because the author's words are those not in inverted commas. **C** is incorrect because inverted commas are not used here to add emphasis.

4 **B** is correct. This is an **inferring** question. You can infer that books about Ireland and the northern hemisphere would be confusing for students who lived in Australia and the southern hemisphere, particularly when the subject was geography. **A**, **C** and **D** are incorrect because there is no evidence that the students were not clever or that the text books were written in Irish or written badly.

5 **B** is correct. This is a **language** question. Goannas don't *improve their minds* *(see line 20)* when they are in a classroom. It is amusing to think that they are learning along with the other children, when they are simply sleeping. **A** is incorrect because, while it is true that goannas like to sleep, this does not make what Henry says amusing. **C** is incorrect because there is no evidence that goannas are afraid of girls. **D** is incorrect because expecting the goanna to be fierce is not what makes Henry's comment amusing.

6 This is a **judgement** question. Modern schools in the bush, for example:

- aren't usually made of bark by someone's father

- don't have the schoolmaster camping in a shelter
- don't use copybooks and pen and ink
- don't use textbooks from Ireland
- don't have goannas sleeping in the classroom.

Scene one (page 87)

1 D **2** B **3** C **4** D **5** C **6** See below

Explanations

1. D is correct. This is a **fact-finding** question. The answer is stated directly in the text. You read *We'll be on the ship for several months* (see lines 9–10). **A** is incorrect because Mrs Rat refers to a ship, not a dinghy. **B** is incorrect because, although they are taking a carriage to the ship, they are preparing for their sea voyage and not the carriage ride. **C** is incorrect because they are going to be at sea, not on the road.
2. **B** is correct. This is a **judgement** question. Mrs Rat tells her husband that he can get used to being without the powders he needs. She tells Harold he'll have to leave his rollerblades behind. You judge that Mrs Rat behaves in a way that is firm minded and tough. **A**, **C** and **D** are incorrect as Mrs Rat does not display any of these qualities.
3. C is correct. This is a **language** question. The word *new-fangled* (see line 16) means something that is the latest fad. Mrs Rat calls Harold's rollerblades *new-fangled* to show her disapproval of his racing about and wearing something she is not familiar with herself. She insists that he leaves them behind, which further confirms her disapproval. (Rollerblades were introduced in the 18th century.) **A** and **B** are incorrect because these attitudes are the opposite of Mrs Rat's attitude towards modern things. **D** is incorrect. Her disapproval is strong but not as powerful as 'horror' implies.
4. D is correct. This is a **synthesis** question. The scene is about the Rat family getting ready to leave their home and go on a sea voyage. **A** and **C** are incorrect as there is no evidence of the scene being about something that is lost or about rats who are blind. **B** is incorrect because the voyage doesn't begin until after this scene.
5. C is correct. This is an **inferring** question. You can work out that this is a play script because its stage directions provide instructions about how the characters should say their lines and what happens on stage. **A**, **B** and **D** are incorrect because other forms of text, such as narratives, include humour, several characters and have a plot.
6. This is a **judgement** question. You judge that Harold enjoys his rollerblades and would want to take them with him. He is a strong character and does things his mother doesn't want him to do and without her knowledge. On the other hand, his mother is strict and likes to be in charge of things. You judge that Harold probably will find a way to take his rollerblades, but it is difficult to be sure.

Caught (page 88)

1 C **2** D **3** B **4** C **5** A **6** See below

Explanations

1. C is correct. This is a **synthesis** question. The text is a poem by Mary Howitt, written in 1829, and would be found in a poetry book with other poems. **A**, **B** and **D** are incorrect because you would be unlikely to find a poem of this kind in a book of plays, a newspaper or a science textbook.
2. D is correct. This is a **synthesis** question. The text gives information about spider webs that would be found in a science text book. **A**, **B** and **C** are incorrect because you would be unlikely to find information of this kind in a poem, a book of plays or a newspaper.
3. **B** is correct. This is an **inferring** question. The spider invites the fly to walk up stairs into the parlour, a room for greeting guests. This makes it sound as though its web is the home of a human being. **A**, **C** and **D** are incorrect because these are not the homes of human beings.
4. C is correct. This is an **inferring** question. You read *For who goes up your winding stair / can ne'er come down again* (see lines 8–9). You infer that the fly knows that, once it steps onto the rungs of the spider's web, it will be unable to escape and will be eaten by the spider. **A**, **B** and **D** are incorrect as there is no evidence that the fly has already had breakfast, has

too much else to do or finds climbing stairs difficult.

5 **A** is correct. This is a **fact-finding** question. The answer is stated directly in the text. You read *it forms a fine, tough thread that is much finer than a human hair* (see lines 13–14). **B** is incorrect because, while the thread is fine, it is not fragile. **C** is incorrect because, while it is tough, it is not thick. **D** is incorrect because it is neither fragile nor flimsy.

6 This is an **inferring** question. You read *The glands produce sticky silk to trap the spider's prey and non-sticky silk to make the spokes and centre of the web* (see lines 14–15). You can infer that spiders use the non-sticky silk as a pathway around the web to avoid getting trapped in the sticky parts. You may also know that spiders usually tiptoe carefully across their webs and groom themselves to scrape off anything that might catch on the web. They do, however, occasionally get trapped in their own webs.

Safe cycling (page 89)

1 C **2** B **3** C **4** A **5** See below

Explanations

1 **C** is correct. This is a **fact-finding** question. The answer is stated directly in the text. You read *The first one told us about bike helmets* (see line 9). **A**, **B** and **D** are incorrect as they are not topics dealt with in the first class.

2 **B** is correct. This is a **synthesis** question. Paragraph two is about bike helmets and safety so this sentence, which is also about bike helmets and safety, would be most relevant there. **A**, **C** and **D** are incorrect as these paragraphs are about different subjects from this sentence.

3 **C** is correct. This is a **language** question. The word *mini* (see line 17) is short for miniature and means a smaller version of traffic lights. **A** and **D** are incorrect because these words describe sizes different from smaller-sized traffic lights. **B** is incorrect because the traffic lights are used for real purposes and are not part of a game.

4 **A** is correct. This is a **judgement** question. You judge that Jess sounds very pleased to learn all there is to learn about bike-riding safety and to practise her riding. She also *highly recommends* (see line 26) the program to everyone. **B** and **D** are incorrect as these attitudes are the opposite of the enthusiasm she shows. **C** is incorrect as there is no evidence that the programme amuses Jess.

5 This is a **judgement** question. Jess learned important things about bike-riding safety that she hadn't known before. She also planned to wear a bike helmet in future, which would improve her chances of not being injured in an accident.

My Shadow (page 90)

1 B **2** C **3** A **4** B **5** D **6** See below

Explanations

1 **B** is correct. This is an **inferring** question. The narrator refers to the shadow as he and says *He is very, very like me from the heels up to the head* (see line 4). You can work out from this that the narrator is a boy. As the narrator has a nurse and plays with other children he must be young. **A**, **C** and **D** are incorrect because there is no evidence that the narrator is a teenager, a young girl or an adult.

2 **C** is correct. This is a **language** question. You read *For he* [the shadow] *sometimes shoots up taller like an india-rubber ball* (see line 8). You work out that the shadow sometimes shoots up to be very tall in the way an india-rubber ball can sometimes bounce up very high. **A** is incorrect. The narrator does not compare the smallness and roundness of the shadow to that of an india-rubber ball. When it gets small, the narrator says the shadow becomes like nothing: [it] *gets so little that there's none of him at all* (see line 9). **B** is incorrect because an india-rubber ball describes the type of rubber the ball is made from, not its place of origin. **D** is incorrect. The narrator does not claim the shadow is fun to play with and does not make this comparison.

3 **A** is correct. This is a **language** question. The narrator is saying that the little shadow doesn't understand the rules of playing with others. He has no idea how he should behave and he embarrasses the narrator by sticking too close. **B**, **C** and **D** are incorrect because how children could, would or do play is not the problem the narrator is complaining about.

4 **B** is correct. This is an **inferring** question. As the narrator says, the usual way for children to grow is very slowly. The little shadow is different because within a short space of time he can be very tall and then very small. **A** is incorrect because children who are not the shadow are the ones who grow very slowly. **C** is incorrect because the little shadow grows tall at times. **D** is incorrect because there is no evidence that he copies the way children grow.

5 **D** is correct. This is a **synthesis** question. The narrator views the little shadow as following him too closely. You can work out that the narrator would never call the little shadow independent as this means 'able to stand on your own two feet' and is the opposite of how the little shadow usually behaves. **A**, **B** and **C** are incorrect. You read *And what can be the use of him is more than I can see* (see line 3), which means that the narrator thinks the little shadow is useless. The narrator also describes the shadow as being a coward and acting in a lazy way *(see lines 12 and 16)*.

6 This is an **inferring** question. The narrator thinks the little shadow stays in bed because he is too lazy to get up. The real reason is because, before dawn when the sun is not yet up, there are no shadows. You can't see your shadow unless there is enough light to create it.

Australian inventors (page 91)

1 B **2** D **3** A **4** B **5** B **6** See below

Explanations

1 **B** is correct. This is an **inferring** question. You work out that Phoebe is counting replies from her classmates when she names the results of her counting. This suggests that what she has been counting is raised hands. **A** is incorrect because people reply, so they must be taking notice. **C** is incorrect because there is no evidence that anyone calls out. **D** is incorrect because it is the opposite of what happens.

2 **D** is correct. This is an **inferring** question. Phoebe implies that, because a large number of her audience has heard of the people she names, they must know a lot about sports people and celebrities. **A** is incorrect because Phoebe includes a celebrity as well as a sports person in her survey that lead to her making this statement. **B** is incorrect because whether or not the audience listened is not what she was talking about. **C** is incorrect because she is implying the opposite of this.

3 **A** is correct. This is a **judgement** question. Phoebe uses abbreviations for the celebrities' names to further convince her audience of how well known they are. She is assuming people will recognise who they are even from their nicknames. **B** is incorrect. Phoebe does not want to confuse her audience; she wants to persuade them to learn more about Australian inventors. **C** is incorrect as Phoebe is not implying that she knows them personally. She couldn't know Bradman as he died in 2001. **D** is incorrect. Phoebe may want to impress or amuse her audience by saying this but the main reason is to reinforce her point about how well known these people are.

4 **B** is correct. This is a **fact-finding** question. The answer is stated directly in the text. You read *I'm not going to tell you about these intriguing inventions. I just hope you'll get interested in Australian inventors and want to find out for yourselves* (see lines 15–18). **A** is incorrect because Phoebe has done her research and knows what they are. **C** is incorrect. Phoebe may like being mysterious but this is not her motive in keeping back information about the inventions. She hopes to intrigue her audience. **D** is incorrect because it is the opposite of what Phoebe hopes will happen.

5 **B** is correct. This is a **language** question. There are several signs that this is a written version of a live speech: *Mmm* (see line 5), for example, is a spoken expression, meaning something similar to 'let me see', which would not appear in a written text. Phoebe conducts a survey as she gives the speech and collates the results on the spot. This is further evidence that her speech is given live to her audience. **A** and **C** are incorrect because only Phoebe is speaking so it can't be classed as a conversation or a discussion. **D** is incorrect. Phoebe is promoting Australian inventors but her speech is not an advertisement. Her audience is Year 3, not the audience of a television program.

6 Answers will vary. This is a **judgement** question. You should look critically at

the strengths and weaknesses of Phoebe's arguments. Your opinion cannot be right or wrong but you do need to give sound reasons to support it.

Brr Brrr. Brr Brrr. (page 92)

1 B **2** B **3** B **4** C **5** D **6** See below

Explanations

1 **B** is correct. This is a **fact-finding** question. The answer is stated directly in the text. You read *I was twelve. … It was 1956 (see lines 15–16)*. This means that Tommy's gran was born twelve years before 1956, which is in 1944. **A** is incorrect because in 1956 Gran was already twelve years old and working in the toy shop. **C** and **D** are incorrect because the text does not say where Tommy's gran was born. She had a part-time job in Melbourne but she may or may not have been born there.

2 **B** is correct. This is a **judgement** question. You judge by the way they ask each other questions and exchange ideas that they are at ease and comfortable with each other. **A**, **C** and **D** are incorrect. There is no evidence of difficulties, hostility or awkwardness in the way they talk together.

3 **B** is correct. This is a **judgement** question. Tommy has asked his mum about her letting him do a paper round. You judge that his Gran wouldn't want to say anything that goes against his mother's views, so she asks what his mother's thoughts are. **A** and **D** are incorrect because there is no evidence that Gran is snoopy or a stickybeak. This is the only question she asks. She tells Tommy things about her own life rather than asking questions about what goes on in Tommy's family. **C** is incorrect because the opposite is true: Gran has plenty to say during their telephone conversation.

4 **C** is correct. This is an **inferring** question. You read *I kept it* [the musical box] *on my windowsill (see line 13)* so you know it can't have been very big. You are also likely to know that the word *mini* means a small version of something. **A**, **B** and **D** are incorrect because they are sizes that would be unlikely to fit on a windowsill.

5 **D** is correct. This is an **inferring** question. You can work out that it was unusual for a toy shop to have a doll hospital attached to it. Gran would not have mentioned this if it was a common practice. **A**, **B** and **C** are incorrect. They are all true statements about the toy shop but none of them include unusual information. There would have been many toy shops in Melbourne at the time, many would have had plenty of toys for sale and some would have had shops next door with a television.

6 This is a **judgement** question. It is likely that Tommy would be encouraged by what his grandmother says. He learns that, when she was young, she worked and earned money which she saved up to buy something that she wanted. She sounds very positive that Tommy will be successful and achieve what he wants, even though it may take some time.

The Wombat (page 93)

1 B **2** C **3** B **4** C **5** A and C
6 See below

Explanations

1 **B** is correct. This is a **language** question. The clue comes from the prefix *quad-*, which means 'four' (e.g. a quadrangle has four sides; quadruple is to multiply by four). Wombats are *quadrupeds (see line 4)*, which means they have four feet. You can tell that **A**, **C** and **D** are incorrect from the context of these words in the text. The word *short-legged (see line 4)* tells you about the length, and not the number of feet, that a wombat has; *gait (see line 9)* refers to a bear's way of walking; and *countenance (see line 17)* refers to the expression on the wombat's face.

2 **C** is correct. This is a **language** question. You read that the natives of Port Jackson called the animal a *Womback (see line 3)*. In 1802 the natives at Port Jackson were First Nations Australian people. **A** is incorrect because the British were not native to New South Wales. **B** is incorrect because the word was used by people native to the area around Port Jackson and so was not made up. **D** is incorrect as there is no evidence in the text that Mr Bass, an English native, used the First Nations word.

3 **B** is correct. This is an **inferring** question. You read *This animal has not any claim to swiftness of foot, as most men could run it down* (see lines 6–7). This suggests that the reason it was easy to catch was that it moved slowly. **A** is incorrect because there is no evidence that Mr Bass was a very swift runner. **C** is incorrect because, although the wombat may have liked being carried, this is not the reason that it was easy to catch. **D** is incorrect because Mr Bass could not have had practice at catching wombats as he is only just finding out about them.

4 **C** is correct. This is a **synthesis** question. The author comments on the mild and gentle disposition of the wombat but points out that it bites and gets furious if it is angered. **A** is incorrect because the author explains that they are not nasty all the time. **B** is incorrect. The author says wombats are *rather inactive* (see line 4), which implies they don't move about much, but this does not mean that they are extremely lazy and slothful. **D** is incorrect as the wombat's behaviour is quite trusting. It showed contentment when being carried along by Mr Bass.

5 **A** and **C** are correct. This is a **fact-finding** question. The answer is stated directly in the text. You read that the wombat lay on Mr Bass's arm *like a child* (see line 16) and that it had the *awkward gait of a bear* (see line 9). **B** is incorrect because the person who behaves like a nurse is Mr Bass, not the wombat. **D** is incorrect because the wombat is not being compared with a grass-eater; it IS a grass-eater.

6 This is a **judgement** question. You read that the book was written in 1804 about the colony of New South Wales. At that time the British would not have been using the metric system so the author uses the earlier term *yards* (see line 14) instead of metres, which came into use much later.

TEXT OVERVIEW GRID

Page	Title	Type of text	Additional teaching points	Writing activity
		Fact-finding questions		
24	The Sydney Harbour Bridge	Informative—report	Built environments; changes in daily living; factual writing	Write a report about a building or other structure that has changed people's lives.
28	Counting	Imaginative—poetry	Numerical order; thinking, saying and relating verbs	Write a poem about yourself or your family using numbers as a way to organise your ideas.
29	Where to get your new pet	Persuasive—letter to the editor	Taking responsibility; forms of address; paragraphing; point of view	Write a letter to the Editor of your local newspaper giving your views about animal shelters as places to get pets.
30	Famous explorers: Bass and Flinders	Informative—report	Natural features of Australia's states and territories; the importance of place in different cultures; biography	Choose an Australian explorer and write about his or her achievements.
31	How to throw a boomerang	Informative—procedure	Procedures; cause and effect; writing in the second person; audience	Write a set of instructions about how to throw a frisbee.
		Synthesis questions		
32	Sea turtles	Informative—report	Environmental issues; features of marine animals; writing reports	Research and write a report about a marine animal's appearance and behaviour.
36	How to make Anzac biscuits	Informative—procedure	Australian symbols; presenting instructions in speech and writing	Have someone film you demonstrating how to make jelly, how to grow flowers or another procedure of your choice.
37	Can I have a worm farm, please?	Persuasive—conversation	Environmental issues; persuasive techniques; family relationships	Write a conversation in which a child persuades a parent to support a cause or do something helpful for the environment.
38	The Voyages of Doctor Dolittle	Imaginative—narrative	Talking animals in stories and film; character development; building tension	Write a story about a character named Doctor Dotoomuch; or review a film version of *Doctor Dolittle*.
39	Bunyips	Informative—report	Mythical beings; sequencing ideas and information; descriptive writing	Invent a mythical creature and describe its behaviour and habits. Include details of reported sightings.
		Inferring questions		
40	Gulliver's Travels	Imaginative—narrative	*Gulliver's Travels* by Johnathan Swift, 1726; comparing sizes and distances; setting and mood in narrative	Write a story about your arrival at a place where the humans are giant-sized.
44	Tell me about Tokyo	Informative—email	Locating Australia's neighbours; communicating electronically	Email a friend living in a neighbouring country to Australia and ask him or her questions about the place and its customs.

Page	Title	Type of text	Additional teaching points	Writing activity
		Inferring questions *(continued)*		
45	How the birds got their colours	Imaginative—narrative	Dreaming stories; thinking and feeling verbs; paragraphing	Create a story about how zebras got their stripes or how elephants got their trunks.
46	Should school uniforms be compulsory?	Persuasive—discussion	Building an argument; emotive language	Present an argument to a familiar audience, either for or against children having mobile phones in the classroom.
47	Whodunnit?	Imaginative—play script	Creatures of the night; play scripts; plot and characterisation	Write your own 'whodunnit' as a play script.
48	Which did you choose?	Informative—conversation	The language and structures of reviews; ways of evaluating texts; expressing opinions	Review a book or film you think your classmates would enjoy.
49	Harmony Day	Persuasive—advertisement	National events; religious celebrations; targeting an audience	Create a poster to advertise a special event such as NAIDOC week, Sorry Day, Hannukah or Chinese New Year.
50	Why do birds fly in a V shape?	Informative—explanation	Writing explanations; paragraphing; topic sentences	Write an explanation as to why humans or animals behave in a particular way, such as why humans yawn or why bees buzz.
51	How Australia got its name	Informative—explanation	Origins of Australian place names; proper nouns	Prepare a talk explaining how places in your local area got their names.
		Language questions		
52	'Ships of the desert'	Informative—report	Changes in transport and effects on daily lives; paragraphing; factual writing	Research and write a brief history of a form of transport such as bullock carts, Cob and Co. coaches, ferries, wool clippers, paddle steamers, cars, trams or trains.
56	My new puppy	Imaginative—diary entry	Taking responsibility; rules; modal verbs and adverbs	Make a list of rules to follow to take care of something you own, such as a new pet, a garden plot or an electronic device.
57	In the olden days	Informative—conversation	Changes in education over time; past, present and future tenses	Imagine a future where you have a grandchild who asks you about your childhood. Write down a conversation you might have.
58	Country life versus city life	Persuasive—speech	The importance of place; different types of settlement; demographic characteristics; point of view	Prepare a speech about the advantages and disadvantages of living where you live now or have lived in the past.
59	City life versus country life	Persuasive—speech	Persuading an audience; logical argument; evaluative language; connectives	Make a visual record of the area where you live (e.g. slide show, video, flipagram) and add music to create a mood for it; or make a slideshow of paintings about life in a particular Australian environment, such as the bush, the city or by the sea.
60	The whistling language	Informative—letter	Different ways of communicating; symbols and their sounds	Research different ways of communicating, such as Morse Code, braille or signing.
61	Jake's jokes	Imaginative—diary entry	Humour; puns; word play	List five of your favourite riddles or jokes.
62	Hang out@Holly's	Persuasive—advertisement	Media texts; advertising techniques; Internet language	Design a webpage advertising a place or a product.

Page	Title	Type of text	Additional teaching points	Writing activity
		Language questions *(continued)*		
63	Dot and the Kangaroo	Imaginative—narrative	Australia's classic authors; characterisation, setting and plot in narrative	Write a story about what happens after Dot climbs into Kangaroo's pouch; or explain to a familiar audience why you like a particular book by an Australian author.
		Judgement questions		
64	Pinocchio	Imaginative—narrative	*Pinocchio*; ethical behaviour; point of view	Write the dialogue of an interview you might have with Pinocchio about why he tells lies.
68	Matilda	Imaginative—poetry	Cautionary tales; humour in rhyme; third-person narrative	Write a limerick about Matilda or her aunt, or write a poem of your own that teaches a moral or lesson.
69	Blogging about bags	Persuasive text—blog	Environmental issues; features of blogs; informal language	Write the first two paragraphs of a blog about something that matters to you.
70	Fire at magic shop	Persuasive—newspaper article	Stereotypes; emotive language; send-ups; irony	Write a newspaper story that is a spoof or send-up.
71	The Swagman	Imaginative—poetry	Symbols of the outback; descriptive language; poetic devices such as simile, metaphor and onomatopoeia	What makes the life of a swagman appealing or unappealing to you? Explain your reasons. Or choose a character from literature or fiction whose way of life appeals to you and explain the reasons for your choice.
72	An advertisement from 1900	Persuasive—visual text	Reading visual texts; advertising techniques; targeting an audience	Design an advertisement for a product using images and only a few words to get your message across.
73	The perils of palm oil	Persuasive—website	Health; sustainability; environmental issues; media texts; point of view	Create a webpage persuading people to eat two portions of fruit and five portions of vegetables daily.
74	Natural wonders	Informative—report	Natural features of Australia's landscape; evaluative language	Choose an Australian natural wonder and explain its significance.
75	Clancy of the Overflow	Imaginative—poetry	Bush ballads; rhythm; rhyme	Write a story about what really happened to Clancy.
		Mixed Questions		
76	Bees	Informative—report	Insects; insect colonies; food chains	Choose an insect, then research and write a report about its predators.
77	Fact file: bees	Informative—report	Conservation; environmental concerns; survival	Prepare a fact file about an endangered animal. Or draw/photograph an insect, label its parts and list major threats to its survival.
78	Just in Time (Part 1)	Imaginative—narrative	Narrative setting; sequencing ideas; connectives	Rewrite a well-known story by changing when and/or where it is set.
79	Just in Time (Part 2)	Imaginative—narrative	Building mood and tension in narrative; relationships; thinking and feeling verbs	Write your own story called 'Just in Time'.
80	First Nations Australian trackers	Informative—report	Racism; honouring contributions to society; summarising	Prepare a Powerpoint presentation about Djungadjinganook and his contributions to society. Or create a Powerpoint presentation about another First Australian who has contributed to Australia's history.

Page	Title	Type of text	Additional teaching points	Writing activity
		Mixed questions *(continued)*		
81	I remember	Informative—personal reflection	Making lists; expressing personal thoughts; time and change	Make a list of memories that you have from when you were very young.
82	Colours and their meanings	Informative—report	Tables; the use of colour in ceremonies, advertising and picture books.	Survey a group of people of different ages and ethnic backgrounds about the associations a particular colour has for them. Present the findings in a table.
83	The Indigenous Round	Informative—report	First Australian communities; diversity of First Nations achievements; symbols	Design a piece of clothing that could be worn at a sporting event in your local area celebrating the contributions of First Australians.
84	Should weekend sport be compulsory?	Persuasive—discussion	Arguments for and against; elaborating on a point; adding emphasis	Prepare the negative case for the topic 'Primary schools should spend more time teaching good manners.'
85	When I grow up	Imaginative—poetry	Growing up; change; voice; rhythm; rhyme schemes	Write a poem in verse with a rhyme scheme abcb about the subject of growing up.
86	Henry Lawson's bush school	Informative—report	Changes in education; biography; interviewing techniques	Interview an older person about his or her school days, and make a list of the similarities and differences from your own school days.
87	Scene one	Imaginative—play script	Different perspectives; family relationships; point of view	Pretend you are Mr, Mrs or Harold Rat and write a speech about your view of the world. Use props and costumes to perform it.
88	Caught	Imaginative—poetry; Informative—report	Dangerous spiders; spiders in art and literature; spiders as totems	Research the way snakes hunt their prey and use the information to write a verse about their behaviour.
89	Safe cycling	Informative—weekly newsletter	Health and safety; rules; symbols and road signs	Make a list of safety rules for you and your family to follow in case of fire, flood or lightning strikes.
90	My Shadow	Imaginative—poetry	Day and night; irony; cause and effect; change	Make a collage of photographs of people's shadows taken at different times of the day. Label the photographs or write captions for them.
91	Australian inventors	Persuasive—speech	Life-changing inventions; technical vocabulary; diagrams; 3D models	Dream up an invention you think the world needs. Draw a diagram of it and label its parts and functions.
92	Brr Brrr. Brr Brrr.	Imaginative—telephone conversation	Listening skills; taking turns; building suspense; audience	Write and perform a one-sided telephone conversation. Provide clues for your audience as to what the other person says.
93	The Wombat	Informative—Report	Australian marsupials; active verbs; word chains; summarising	Research how to get help for an injured animal in your state or territory from WIRES or another wildlife rescue group. Design a fridge magnet with key information for your area.

Notes